VOICES FROM THE DESERT

Hugh MacMahon completed his Asian studies in Ottawa, Canada. He has spent most of his life in Korea and China exploring the roots of Asian culture and the influence they still have on the development of some of the world's most vibrant nations. Upon returning to Ireland he began examining his own national heritage to identify its sources and what they might have to offer society today. He has written on culture for a number of Korean magazines and previously published *Guest From The West* and *The Scrutable Oriental.*

VOICES FROM THE DESERT

The Lost Legacy of the Skelligs

HUGH MACMAHON

columba
BOOKS

First published in 2021 by

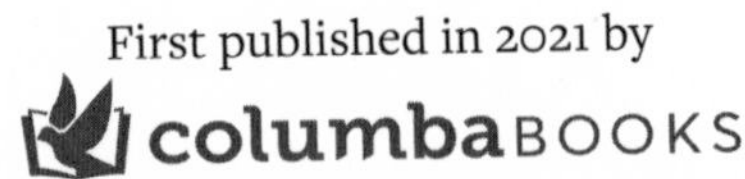

Block 3b, Bracken Business Park,

Bracken Road, Sandyford,Dublin 18, D18 K277

www.columbabooks.com

ISBN: 978-1-78218-3808

Set in Freight Text Pro and Freight Sans Pro 11.5/15.5

Cover and book design by Alba Esteban | Columba Books

Frontcover image: Skellig Sunset, with atlantic waves bracing St Finan's Bay, Skellig Michael and Skellig Beag in the distance, Iveragh Peninsula, Co Kerry. Photo:Valerie O'Sullivan.

Backcover image: Johannes Cassianus Cassianus, Liber Chronicarum, Woodcut. Rijksmuseum, CCo, via Wikimedia Commons.

Printed by L&C, Poland.

‘It is a wretched thing to profess to learn any art
or pursuit and never to arrive at perfection in it.’

Abba John

Contents

Introduction

The Vikings who stormed up the narrow tracks to the monastic cells on the top of the Skellig Rocks in AD 823 were disappointed and baffled. There was nothing to plunder – the few men who lived there owned nothing but the bare necessities for life. If there was one surprise, in an illiterate age, it was the number of books they found.

What sort of men would live there? Were they criminals in exile or were they guarding something valuable? If the raiders had been able to read the books found there they might have discovered the answer. Instead they took the men off the island rock and sold them as slaves. One old monk, Etgal, seemed to be the leader and perhaps worth ransoming. When nothing came of that they let him die of starvation.

The books found on the Skelligs were either written by or referred to a man named John Cassian. More than a thousand years later, if anyone still wants to know why the monks were on the Skelligs, how they spent their days and what they talked about among themselves, the answers can be found in what Cassian wrote.

How these books came to be written, how they got to Ireland and what they have to say about attitudes to life, then and now, are related here.

One volume was an account of the journey made by John Cassian and a companion across the deserts of Egypt in 385 to visit the hermitages and monasteries of revered monks and learn from their way of life. It is written in a question-and-answer interview style, with comments on the people they met, local customs and their own efforts to practise what impressed them.

The second book was written at the request of a local bishop as a guide for the monastic movement that was beginning to spread across Europe, eventually reaching as far as Ireland. It laid out rules and directions for running a community according to the ideals and practices of the Desert Fathers and Mothers of Egypt.

These two books, in Latin, became essential reading for monks, including those on the Skelligs. As John Ryan states in his *Irish Monasticism,* 'To the Irish mind an illiterate monk was a contradiction in terms.'

Today these volumes offer unique insights into the lives of people who lived in an era which, until recently, was considered 'dark' because of the lack of records. When the Vikings attacked the Skelligs Ireland was already dotted with hermitages and monasteries that gave names to their localities. Those monasteries were following the guidelines developed by Cassian and other pioneers. Eventually they led to Ireland's reputation as an 'island of saints and scholars'.

Another reason for reading Cassian today is his account of the beliefs and practices of the pre-institutional Christian Church. Many will be surprised at what they read. The monks were not fleeing the world, but rather saw themselves as responding to a challenge. They were not punishing themselves but testing the limits of their abilities. They left home, comforts and social ambition to learn how to deal with their human weaknesses by facing up to the most ambitious of human goals. The majority of them were moderate, educated people, conscious of their individuality and prepared to test their convictions.

If Cassian's writings are such a unique and valuable insight into the lifestyle and thinking of the early Irish and European educated class, why are they not better known and utilised?

There are at least two good reasons.

As we listen in to each discussion or 'conference' we can picture Cassian with his notebook, carefully jotting down every word spoken by the revered Elder, or 'Abba'. His companion, Germanus, intervenes with the kind of questions anyone would like to ask and the Abba replies with patience. During such informal encounters, which often went on into the night, the flow of words and ideas wander. At times the Abba is precise and analytical. Three or four aspects of the question are identified and dealt with in turn. At other times they launch out into a winding tour, pausing for anecdotes and biblical quotations, either to illustrate the point or give it authority. (There are over 1,500 biblical quotations in the Conferences.) As a result the chapters are lengthy – after a few pages the reader's energy and patience will be tested. The modern reader might wish they had stuck to one point and spelt it out in less detail.

The entire Conferences cover 470 pages. In the condensed version that follows I have attempted to highlight the main topic of each discussion, using the speaker's own thinking and language as much as possible. A short commentary is added to clarify the background and suggest some implications. It is hoped that readers will be moved to explore the original text in full.

The second reason why Cassian's writings attracted so little attention outside monastic libraries is that his reputation was slightly tainted by the accusation that he favoured Pelagianism and gave too much credit to the role of free will. As a monk he accepted the key role played by God in drawing people to a deeper awareness of what a human can achieve, yet he did not want to concede that human efforts played no part in making a commitment to that journey and seeking progress in it. Finding acceptable words to express a 'middle way' that balanced God's role and that of the individual was not easy, despite his best efforts.

Today Cassian's views are widely accepted, in Catholic circles at least, but for many centuries the topic remained so sensitive that few would risk raising it in public for fear of being seen as favouring one side or the other. As a result, translations of the Conferences into English were few and incomplete. The nineteenth-century versions used slightly dated language and omit two conferences (12 and 22) because their subject matter was of a sensitive sexual nature. Recent translations and commentaries have sought to remedy this.

Before going any further, who were Cassian and Germanus, and in what sort of world were they living?

Cassian

John Cassian was born around AD 360 to wealthy parents in Scythia Minor, now Romania. Educated in Latin and Greek, at around the age of twenty he left home with his companion Germanus to further his studies in Palestine. After five years in a hermitage near Bethlehem they began to visit the monks in the Scete desert in Egypt, staying there until 392. Following a short visit to their 'home' monastery near Bethlehem, they returned to Egypt and remained there until 399.

In that year Cassian and Germanus became involved in a theological controversy. They went to Alexandria to consult with the Patriarch, but when no agreement could be reached they had to flee the region with 300 other monks.

They went on to Constantinople where they appealed to the Patriarch, John Chrysostom, for protection. From there they went on to Rome to report to Pope Innocent l.

While in Rome Cassian was ordained priest and accepted an invitation to establish an Egyptian-style monastery in southern Gaul, near Marseilles. In 415 he founded the Abbey of St Victor for men and that of St Sauveur for women. These abbeys became the model for later generations in Europe, including Ireland.

Around 420, at the request of a bishop wishing to establish a community of monks, Cassian wrote two major spiritual works, *The Institutes* and *Conferences of the Desert Fathers*. The *Institutes* dealt with the external affairs of monastic communities such as clothing, prayer and rules of monastic life. The *Conferences* were less formal and intended for 'the training of the inner man and the perfection of the heart'.

Cassian developed close ties with the monastery on the Island of Lérins, where it is said St Patrick studied before going to Ireland.

Towards the end of his life John Cassian's final writing task was a *Treatise Against Nestorius*. It was composed in 430 as a brief for the Pope, explaining the issues in Nestorius's Christology as preparation for what became the Third Ecumenical Council.

Cassian died in 435 at Marseille. Though he had little to say about himself, his writings reveal a man of exceptional ability and humanity.

He was educated in the abstract thinking of Plato and Socrates, the self-sufficiency of the Cynics and the Stoics' suppression of passions for a life of right reason. He was equally at home with the Old and New Testaments, the teaching of the early theologians and pioneering monks such as Anthony and Macarius.

When a question was posed in a conference, it was answered by breaking it down into its component parts and evaluating these systematically on the basis of reason, scripture and the inherited tradition.

Human weaknesses were diagnosed according to the methods used by medical experts of that time to classify physical symptoms, tracing them to their origin in an organ or other part of the body and suggesting treatment. Moral failings and guilt were tracked back to one of eight basic sources in the psyche and dealt with appropriately.

Cassian saw monks as soldiers or athletes in training for challenging contests. Those images were first proposed in the Gospels and by St Paul, but for the monks they had an immediate significance. Alone in their cells they had to fight their inner vulnerabilities as well as thoughts or illusions that seemed to come from outside them and have a maliciousness of their own.

Just as athletes gave up comforts and relationships, and willingly endured self-imposed hardship to earn a prize, monks too were prepared to do what was necessary to achieve their goal.

Cassian's writings are still regarded as classics on the spiritual life. Not only was he observant and moderate, but he also, as observed by the historian Owen Chadwick, 'possessed a very penetrating and rare ability for psychological analysis'.

Germanus

Less is known about Germanus. Born in the mid-fourth century, probably in the diocese of Tomis in what is now Romania, Germanus may have been related to John Cassian. He entered a local monastery as an ascetic while still a young man and became the travel companion, spiritual father and teacher of John Cassian, instructing him in monastic perfection. They lived at one of the monasteries of Dacia Pontica for a short time before going to Bethlehem.

Germanus was ordained priest in 399 when they were in Constantinople. He spent the rest of his life in a monastery, most likely in Dacia Pontica, where he died early in the fifth century. He was declared a saint in the Eastern Church, as was John Cassian.

Though older and more experienced than Cassian, it was Germanus who often interrupted the conferences to ask personal questions, which brought the discussions down to earth.

Among his concerns was the question whether separation from society, though providing opportunities to be closer to God, did not contradict the Christian duty to help others, seek justice and practise kindness.

He was aware of his personal limitations and asked whether the ideals being set before them were not too much to expect from humans.

He also asked: If God's help is essential for us to make progress, do our own efforts have little or no meaning and value? How can we love God if we are also told to fear God?

Such questions helped to develop the discussion but also show an awareness of the challenging demands being put before them, the questions that had to be answered and the spiritual and physical effort that was required.

Origins of the Monastic Movement

In Conference 11, Abba Piamun gives the account of the Desert Fathers and Mothers of the development of Christian monasticism, seeing it as an extension of the spirit and life of the early Christian communities.

The movement grew at the end of the third century, with Paul of Thebes (226–341) and Anthony the Great (252–356) being regarded as leading figures. Anthony was the first to go alone into the wilderness. Thanks to a popular biography by Athanasius of Alexandria he became known as 'the father of all monks'. There are numerous references to him in the *Conferences.* Today Irish memories of Paul and Anthony are preserved on the tenth-century High Cross at Monasterboice on which both are depicted.

Within Anthony's lifetime, a number of hermits gathered around the monk Macarius at Kellia in 328, living in a loosely connected brotherhood. Pachomius (292–348), a former Roman soldier, took the next step and set up the first recognised monastic community (cenobium). In 323 he founded a monastic cloister in Tabennisi, north of Thebes, combining houses of thirty to forty monks, each with its own superior (Abba). The intention was to bring together individual ascetics who did not have the will or physical ability to live a solitary existence in the desert. This method of monastic organisation was called cenobitic or 'communal'.

Pachomius was so successful he was called upon to help organise new cenobia, and by the time he died in 346 there were thought to be 3,000 such communities dotted around Egypt, especially in the Thebaid.

In the Nitrian desert a group of Greek-influenced monks joined Evagrius Ponticus (345–399). John Cassian was one of his disciples, and it was from the monks there that he gathered the information and experiences that form his *Conferences and Institutes.*

While monasticism developed its own traditions in the east of the Roman Empire, in the west its introduction is credited to Martin of Tours. A Roman soldier, he gave up military life to be a disciple of the scholarly Hilary of Poitiers (310–367), whose studies of Old and New Testament writings led to his abandoning Neoplatonism for Christianity. Encouraged by Hilary, he founded a hermitage near Poitiers that was to become famous as Ligugé Abbey, the oldest monastery in Europe.

In 371 Martin was made bishop of Tours but lived as a hermit outside the city in the monastery of Marmoutier. His cell was a wooden hut, and around it his disciples, who soon numbered eighty, lived in caves and huts. It became a colony of hermits rather than a single integrated community. This type of simple life, based on the Egyptian example, spread so rapidly that 2,000 monks were present at Martin's funeral.

Equally important for Ireland was the monastery of Lérins, which gave to the Church of Gaul some of its most famous bishops and saints. John Cassian settled at Lérins for a time, and it was from there that he founded the great Abbey of St Victor of Marseilles.

A rule for monastic life, based on Cassian, was drawn up by Columbanus of Bangor (540–615) for the monasteries he founded in northern Europe. It introduced the Irish practices of private confession, mission preaching and sharing learning. However, even in Columbanus's own monasteries in Europe, this rule was soon replaced by the more temperate Rule of Benedict of Nursia.

Columbanus's Rule, perhaps because of its closeness to the spirit of Cassian, was criticised for its demanding standards, strict discipline and harsh austerities. In comparison the Benedictine Rule was considered more moderate and reasonable. It did not expect the abbot to be a charismatic figure and paid more attention to the administrative structures than did the Irish system, which focused on spiritual practices. While the heroic standards expected by the Egyptian monks suited the passionate spirit of the Celts, a need to moderate them was felt on the continent.

Benedict (480–547) had been living as a solitary in a cave near Subiaco, Italy, when he was asked to lead a group of hermits wishing to change to the monastic style of Pachomius by living in community. Between the years 530 and 560 he wrote his Rule, a remarkable document that has influenced European civilisation and the spiritual lives of countless committed men and women.

In Ireland Benedictine foundations were slow to develop. While three of the first bishops of Dublin between 1028 and 1095 were Benedictines, they were subject to Canterbury and supported by the Norse of Dublin. After that the Benedictine order was rarely mentioned until recent times, when its spiritual influence has become significant. The old Irish monastic traditions survived up to the twelfth century, when the Irish Church began to adapt to the system of dioceses, parishes and reformed monastic orders familiar elsewhere in Europe. Traces of the Irish enthusiasm for heroic and demanding expressions of faith remain in the barefoot pilgrimage on Croagh Patrick on Reek Sunday and in doing the patterns at Lough Derg.

The earliest Desert Mother on record is Amma Syncletica of Alexandria (270–350). After the death of her parents she sold off her family wealth and gave it to the poor. She took up the life of a hermit, living in a graveyard. Soon a community gathered around her. Twenty-seven 'sayings' are attributed to her in the 'Sayings of the Desert Fathers' (first compiled at the end of the fourth century). Among them is her assertion that asceticism is not an end in itself.

Theodora of Alexandria became the Amma of a monastic community near her native city. It is said that prior to that she dressed as a man in order to join a community of monks. Theodora was known for her humility, and Bishop Theophilus of Alexandria came to her for counsel.

Melania the Elder (350–417) was born in Spain to a family of consular rank. She was widowed at an early age and went on pilgrimage to the Nitrian Desert. Inspired by what she saw there, she founded a convent in Jerusalem with a community of fifty and became an acquaintance of the scholar-monks Macarius and Jerome. Her granddaughter, Melania the Younger, followed her example and was also a noted monastic founder.

Paula of Rome (347–404) was the daughter of an ancient senatorial family. Widowed at the age of thirty-two, under the influence of a fellow Roman, St Marcella, she gave up her privileged life and set out on a pilgrimage to the Holy Land. Among her travel companions was St Jerome. Both of them were to found monasteries in Bethlehem.

Paula maintained her ascetic devotion through her intensive studies of the Old and New Testaments, assisting Jerome in his translation of the Bible from Hebrew and Greek into Latin.

The Irish Tradition

St Martin of Tours, thanks to a widely read biography by Sulpicius Severus, is remembered for cutting his military cloak in two with his sword and giving half of it to a ragged beggar in winter. In Ireland it was his life as a bishop-hermit that inspired many to follow his example and launch an indigenous monastic system.

His monastery at Marmoûtiers was the training ground for many Celtic missionaries. St Patrick was said to have been his nephew and to have spent time there. St Ninian (360–432), whose Candida Casa in Scotland was familiar to Irish scholars, was one of his disciples, and brought back a deep respect for his teacher.

Martin's name surfaces in many documents from that time. *The Life of Columbanus* by Jonas relates how the Irish saint, in his travels though France, requested an opportunity to pray at the tomb of St Martin. An Irish palimpsest sacramentary from the mid-seventh century contains the text of a mass for St Martin. In his *Life of Columba of Iona*, Adamnán mentions that St Martin was commemorated during Mass at Iona.

One of those who studied at Martin's monastery was Finnian of Clonard (470–549). He left Ireland after his initial studies and went to Gaul to join the community at Tours. He later spent a number of years at monasteries in Wales. On his return to Ireland he visited Brigid in Kildare and is said to have lived for a while in a cell on the Skelligs. He finally settled at Clonard in Meath, building a cell and church of wattle.

He soon attracted disciples and set up a school based on the teachings of the Desert Fathers, becoming known as the 'tutor of the saints of Ireland'. Among the 3,000 students that gathered there were the 'Twelve Apostles of Ireland', who in turn, founded monasteries across the island and beyond. Colum of Derry (521–597) brought his Irish or Celtic monastic system to northern Britain. Columbanus of Bangor (540–615) brought it to France, Austria, Switzerland and Italy.

Finnian's Twelve Apostles of Ireland changed the landscape of the country. Today there are over a hundred towns and villages whose name begins with 'Kil', derived from the old Irish word 'cell', borrowed from the Latin 'cellae'. While the word also came to denote a church or graveyard, the original name points to the cell or residence of the holy person whose name is associated with the district. Another place name, dysert, comes from 'desert'. This was where the local holy person went to practise the life of a hermit, escaping from the increasing demands of life in the monastery.

In Ireland, the most famous 'Amma' or Abbess was Brigid of Kildare (451–525). Her father was said to have been an early convert of St Patrick and, according to the Book of Armagh, 'Between St Patrick and St Brigid, the pillars of the Irish people, there was so great a friendship of charity that they had but one heart and one mind.'

The fact that in 480, along with six companions, Brigid established a monastery for women in Kildare indicates how quickly the monastic system was spreading in Ireland. She also founded a community of men, inviting the hermit Conleth from nearby Newbridge, to help her pastor them. Among her disciples was Tigernach from Oriel, who visited her on his way back from Rome and Candida Casa before establishing a monastery in Clones.

Brigid's school in Kildare became famous for its artists who made beautiful chalices and other metal objects needed in the church, as well as the ornamentation of missals, gospels and psalters. It became a centre of religion and learning, developing into a prestigious cathedral city. Brigid herself is one of the patron saints of Ireland.

Moninne of Killeavy, a contemporary and friend of Brigid, had 'received the veil' from St Patrick. She founded a monastery near Newry. Fourteen churches in Ireland, England and Scotland are attributed to her activities.

In the west of the country, St Ita of Killeedy (d. 570) was a renowned teacher and was known as the 'foster mother of the Saints of Ireland'.

Other Irish foundress 'Ammas' include Gobnait of Cork, Arraght of Sligo, Cocha of Kilcock, Bronagh of Down and Ciara of Cork.

There were also a number of 'Double Monasteries' with both male and female members. They lived apart but gathered in the same church for Mass and the Office and had the same superior.

The Conferences

It is now time to turn to the text of the discussions or 'conferences' themselves.

The content of each conference is abridged to focus on the main topic and how it was treated. The thoughts expressed are those of the Elder interviewed and their own articulation is retained as much as possible.

A short commentary follows to give some background information and explore implications for today.

The Conclusion to the book will seek to summarise John Cassian's influence.

CONFERENCE 1

Selfless or Selfish?

In AD 384 John Cassian, at the age of twenty-four, along with his slightly older friend Germanus, set out from their monastery in Bethlehem to interview the reclusive monks of the Egyptian deserts. The two learned young men felt they were sufficiently knowledgeable and practised in the basics of Christianity, and were now ready to learn directly from the 'Desert Masters', the experts in spiritual well-being, how to make further progress.

Our first meeting In the Scete desert was with the Abba Moses, famed for his practical advice and advanced in contemplation. At the beginning the Abba questioned our sincerity but, once assured of our genuine interest, he agreed to a discussion. He posed the first question.

Moses: Everyone has a goal in mind that drives them to action, whether it is the farmer labouring in the field, the merchant taking risks or the soldier scorning danger.

Our calling has its own objectives and to achieve them we make strenuous efforts without getting tired. Rather, we take delight in them. Fasting is not a trial for us, vigils are welcome gifts and constant meditation on the scriptures never drains our energies. You yourselves have left your loved ones, fatherland and the delights of this world to come to us, plain and simple folk that we are. Why did you make this journey?

We were slow to offer an answer but finally stated it was for the sake of the kingdom of heaven.

Moses: Good, you have spoken well of the ultimate goal. But what should be our immediate goal?

We were not sure. That was what we came to find out.

Moses: If we do not know where we are going, we can easily get lost. The immediate goal is purity of heart ('Blessed are the pure in heart, they shall see God.' Matthew 5:8). Let us keep our eye on that goal all the time or we will get lost.

Whatever can direct us towards that goal is to be sought with all our ability, and what deters us from it is to be avoided and considered harmful.

If you are not clear about what you are looking for you might give up all your worldly goods to come to live in the desert but end up allowing yourself to get worked up over minor things – a missing knife, pencil or book. Those who achieve a pure heart never end up anxious about such small matters. As the apostle Paul said, it is no use giving up all your goods to feed the poor if you do not have true charity, that is, purity of heart.

We monks seek the solitude of the desert and submit to fasting, vigils, labour, minimum clothing and studies so that our hearts might not be disturbed. With the help of these practices we can overcome vexations, anger and passions. However, what we gain from fasting will not make up for what we lose by being angry. Our self-denial is not perfection, it is only an aid to perfection.

Our constant goal is to seek God and heavenly things. Take the story of Martha and Mary in the Gospels. When Jesus visited them, Martha performed a worthy service by preparing food for him and his disciples. Mary, meanwhile, was intent on gaining spiritual instruction and sat close to the feet of Jesus. When Martha complained and looked for Mary's help, Jesus said, 'Martha, Martha, you are anxious and troubled about many things but few things are needed. Mary has chosen the better part' (Luke 10:41).

The chief good consists in meditation, that is, divine contemplation. All other virtues are in second place, even if they are excellent and necessary.

Germanus: What about fasting, studying the scriptures, works of mercy, justice, piety and kindness? Did the Lord not say, 'Come into the Kingdom, you blessed of my Father' to those who fed him in the hungry and the thirsty?

Moses: What you call works of charity and mercy are indeed needful while inequalities and differences of conditions continue to exist in society. However, even now we should not get caught up in them unless there is a large proportion of poor, needy and sick folk among us. Such destitution is brought about by the wickedness of men – those who have grasped and kept for their own use things that were granted to all by the Creator.

As long as such disparity lasts, working for the needy remains necessary and will bring the promised reward. However, of their nature such activities will come to an end when equality reigns in the life to come and we will move from practical works of mercy to the love of God and contemplation of spiritual things.

St Paul said that even the higher gifts of the Holy Spirit such as prophecy, speaking in tongues and growth in knowledge will all pass away and charity alone will abide for ever. All gifts are given for a time to be used as needs require, but when this present order ends they will pass away. Love alone will never disappear.

Love is our mainstay in this world and when the burden of bodily needs is cast off, it will continue with far greater vigour and excellence. It will never be weakened by any defect.

Germanus: What if a brother or a sick person or a stranger comes to us during our time of prayer or contemplation? Can they be ignored? We also need time to attend to our physical needs. How can the mind be always focused on the incomprehensible God?

Moses: It is impossible for us as humans to be always immersed in God. But we should always be aware of what our goal is, rejoicing when we are actively seeking it and sad when we are distracted by some physical need. Everything depends on this inward frame of mind.

When we are thinking of nothing but God, then 'the kingdom of God is within us'. When we are caught up in material concerns we are living in another kingdom. What is specially peculiar and appropriate to true blessedness is constant calm and eternal joy. Jesus came so that the kingdom of God would replace the kingdom of this world.

While continuing to live in the body a person should accept that human reality and commit to it, but also be aware of the eternal world where they will be united with him whose servant they are in this life. The kingdom of God is attained by the practice of purity of heart and spiritual knowledge. When Jesus on the cross said to the man crucified beside him, 'Today you will be with me in paradise', he indicated that after separation from the body the soul is not deprived of perception or consciousness. It is madness to even think that the nobler part of man, in which the image and likeness of God exist, will become insensible.

This contemplation of God is achieved in a variety of ways. We not only discover God by admitting his incomprehensible essence, which still lies hid in the hope of the promise, but we see him through the greatness of his creation, the consideration of his justice and the aid of his daily providence. It is practised when, with pure minds, we contemplate what he has done with his saints in every generation, when with trembling hearts we admire his power with which he governs, directs and rules all things; the vastness of his knowledge; and that eye of his from which no secret of the heart can be hid. We practise it when we consider the sands of the sea and the number of the waves measured by him and known to him, when in our wonder we think that the drops of rain, the days and hours of the ages, and all things past and future are present in his knowledge. We experience it when we gaze in unbounded admiration on that ineffable mercy of his, which, with unwearied patience, endures countless sins that are this very moment being committed under his very eyes ...

Germanus: What about when we are distracted? Even against our will, idle thoughts steal upon us that are not only difficult to drive away but even to grasp and seize.

Moses: It is impossible for the mind not to be approached by thoughts but it is in the power of every earnest person either to admit them or to reject them. We should not be blaming other people or evil spirits, we have our own free will.

Reading the scriptures and meditating give us opportunities for spiritual recollection; singing psalms raises feelings of compunction; earnest vigils, fasts and prayer bring the mind low and lead from earthly things to contemplation of things celestial and prevent carelessness creeping in.

Our heart is like a mill. What it produces depends on what is put into it. If it is fed with the scriptures, spiritual thoughts will emerge. If it is fed with gossip and worldly concerns, the results will be harmful.

There are three origins to our thoughts: God, the Devil and ourselves.

Those that are from God come when we are enlightened by the Holy Spirit or put to shame by our laziness.

Those from the Devil are temptations to sinful pleasures or the deceitful portraying of evil as good.

Those from within us arise when we needlessly go back over past actions or what someone said or did to us.

We need to examine our thoughts to see where they originated. Does what occupies our mind come from the Spirit or is it based on some worldly philosophy or superstition? 'Believe not every spirit, but prove the spirits whether they are of God' (1 John 4:1.) Wrong interpretations of scripture can lead us away from the monastic life.

Think of how coinage is examined to see whether it is genuine or counterfeit.

First we check whether it is solid gold or just painted deceptively on the outside. Then we look to see whether it bears the image of the true king. We test the weight, whether it is heavy with good for all or light with human display or novelty. Finally, we put it on the public balance to see whether it is up to the standard set by the apostles and prophets.

***

Both of us were so caught up in this discussion that we wanted it to continue, but Abba Moses reminded us it was already night. He was impressed by our interest in discerning between what was good and what was harmful, but it was too late in the evening to go further into such an important topic. He advised us to take some rest.

We put our bundles under our heads to use as pillows, and at the bidding of the old man we settled ourselves down to sleep in deep stillness, both excited with delight at the conference we had held, and buoyed up with hope of the promised discussion.

Abba Moses begins in typical desert style by challenging the visitors about their intentions. Why did you come here? What do you want to do with your life? If a person is not clear about what they want from the start they will easily be sidetracked and frustrated.

The young men venture to suggest they are seeking the Kingdom of God, but Moses says that is too vague; people need a clear and immediate objective to energise and guide them.

Their goal should be 'purity of heart'. In practice this means getting rid of anything that might come between you and God and prevent you seeing God clearly. If you take your eye off this goal you will never make any progress.

He assures them that what they get in return is beyond anything they can imagine but it means everything else must take second place in their lives. It is a message that will keep coming up.

The young men are prepared to give up other ambitions and accept solitude, fasting, vigils and labour if that helps them to overcome their weaknesses, but they also have questions that seem quite reasonable.

Did such complete dedication not cut them off completely from the world? The gospels said that involvement in society is an essential part of making the Kingdom a reality. Are those involved in a family and making a contribution to society not as much a part of the Kingdom as those isolating themselves to seek only God and heavenly things?

In reply, Moses reminds them of the Martha/Mary story in the Bible, which suggests that time devoted to deepening one's relationship with God was 'better' than actively responding to the needs of others.

Abba Moses sees this as indicating that the services we can provide in this life are limited, and they will not be needed in the next. What begins in this life but will endure is our relationship with God. That is what we should be concentrating on.

However, Cassian and Germanus are not completely satisfied with that interpretation of the gospel. How to balance the interior search with a gospel-inspired concern for others is a topic that will emerge again in later conferences. A solution can be seen in

Cassian's own life. After his years in the desert he went on to be a peacemaker between disputing theologians, adviser to a pope and founder of a monastery that was to influence civilisation in the western world.

Many of those trained in the desert later became teachers, bishops and community leaders; others remained to build on their initial experiences and become elders qualified to advise and guide the next generation.

Whether the monks on the Skelligs were permanent residents or short-term practitioners we cannot be sure, but many among the thousands who studied at Finnian's Clonard went on to found monasteries in Ireland and beyond, contributing to the life of people. The resolute efforts of the monks to experience the sacred would open a wider world and deepen the self-evaluation of the people among whom they lived.

CONFERENCE 2

Weighing Options

The following morning we met with Abba Moses again, as arranged. Moses remarked on how impressed he was by our enthusiasm and how he looked forward to our discussion.

Moses: Those who led the way for us attached great importance to discernment. When I was still a young boy, some older monks came to the legendary holy Father Anthony in the Thebaid desert to ask him about perfection. Their discussion went on all through the day and night that followed. Each gave his opinion of what kept the seeker on the right path.

Some said it was fasts and vigils, others that it was in despising all earthly things, others that it was complete withdrawal from the world. A number held it was the duty of charity and kindness, as the Lord promised the kingdom to those who practised it.

The night was coming to an end when Anthony himself spoke. He said, 'All these things which you have mentioned are indeed needful, and helpful to those who are thirsting for God. But from experience we know that some who practised them could not keep their efforts up and abandoned the monastic life. For while those praiseworthy virtues abounded in them, discretion alone was wanting and prevented them from continuing to the end.'

By discretion he meant the 'eye' that keeps one going in the right direction.

I have heard about, and seen, many such downfalls myself.

There was an old man, Heron, who had lived a life of strict severity in the desert for fifty years. He would not even join the others at Easter in case it was a sign that he was lowering his principles. Then, not long ago, he had the illusion that if he jumped into a deep well he would have nothing to fear. He would be saved because of the holiness of his life.

When his neighbours finally got him out he was almost dead and he passed away three days later.

Then there were the two monks in the Thebaid who, journeying through the desert, were determined not to take any food with them, relying on what the Lord would provide. When they got to the point where they were fainting from hunger they met some nomads who offered them food. One received it with gratitude, as coming from the Lord, while the other refused it because it was offered to him by pagans. He died of starvation.

Another example was the monk in Mesopotamia who practised extreme fasts but was deceived by dreams that convinced him that non-Christians enjoyed a greater reward than those who believed.

None of these would have been so miserably deceived if they had endeavoured to obtain the power of discernment.

Germanus: Discernment is indeed important in keeping the seeker on the right road. How can it be achieved?

Moses: Discernment can be gained only by true humility. We cannot rely entirely on our own judgement and should submit important questions to the judgement and advice of the elders.

As a young man the Abbot Serapion spent time with Abbot Theonas. Each day at the ninth hour he supped with the old man and secretly hid a biscuit in his dress to eat later when he was hungry. He felt guilty about it but could not give up the habit. One day, when the old man was addressing a group of visitors, he spoke about gluttony and secret thoughts. Serapion was so overcome he blurted out his secret. The old man responded, 'Have faith, my child. Without any words of mine, your confession frees you from this slavery. For you have triumphed over your adversary and laid him low by your confession, which more than makes up for the way you were overthrown by him.'

No one is more deceived than when he is persuaded by himself to despise the counsel of the Elders and rely on his own opinion and judgement.

In all walks of life there is need for a teacher to show the way to be followed. We should follow the footsteps of the Elders with the utmost care and bring to them every doubt that rises in our hearts by removing the veil of shame.

Germanus: There was a young man who confessed his weakness to an Elder, who immediately chided him severely and with great indignation, causing him great shame and a reluctance to confess after that.

Moses: Just as all young men are not alike in fervour of spirit, so not all old men are equally perfect and excellent. The true value of Elders is not to be measured by their grey hairs but by the efforts they made in their youth to achieve perfection and what they learnt from the experience. Unhappily there are many who pass their old age in a lukewarmness that they contracted in youth and obtained authority not from the maturity of their character but simply from the number of their years.

There once was an Elder who publicly reprimanded a youth and almost forced him to leave the monastery, only to be temped himself and disgraced before the brethren.

Extremes are to be avoided. Excessive fasting and gluttony come to the same thing. Unlimited vigils are as harmful to a monk as too much sleep.

Your compatriot Benjamin showed his lack of discretion by fasting completely for two days and then greedily filling his stomach with a double portion on the third day. Eventually he left the desert and went back to his studies of philosophy.

Germanus: What then are the extremes to be avoided when fasting?

Moses: This question has often been discussed and in great detail. It is now proposed that monks eat only two biscuits of bread a day, together weighing less than a pound.

Germanus: We are surprised. It seems very liberal and would be no bother to us. [A pound of bread would be the equivalent of a medium-sized loaf.]

Moses: When you are engaged in the practice of minimising your diet you should never change the daily intake, even when visitors come. After a large meal the body can survive on less than usual for the next few days and the rhythm will be broken. Beware, the regular fast is hard to keep!

The sensible rule is for everyone to allow themselves food according to the requirements of their strength or bodily frame and not for the satisfactory feeling of repletion. The Elders agree that daily hunger should go hand in hand with our daily meals, preserving both body and soul in the same condition and not allowing the mind either to faint through weariness from fasting nor to be oppressed by over-eating.

Germanus: What should we do when visitors come? If we do not offer them something it would seem like a lack of courtesy.

Moses: When you offer food to a brother it would be ridiculous not to share food with them. Keep back one of the biscuits from the regular meal in case visitors come in the evening. Then, if visitors come, it could be eaten with them. If not, it should be eaten anyhow. It is the aim or reason for what you do that is important.

Eating at the ninth hour [3.00 pm] is a convenient and suitable time. It allows the body and mind to be refreshed and ready for evening prayers as the food will have been fully digested.

***

The discussion ended at this point but after these two sessions we believed we had learned something 'clearer than daylight'. Up till then, we had not been lacking in effort and enthusiasm in our search for perfection but Abba Moses had provided us with a clearer understanding of our ultimate aim and of the purity of heart that would provide us with a strong sense of direction.

◇◇◇

In the previous conference Abba Moses had stressed the importance of discernment, or being able to distinguish what is useful from what is harmful. He did so as a doctor might, listing three sources from which thoughts can come and four ways of checking their value.

The three possible sources are God, the Devil or ourselves.

- What comes from God are ideas or insights that unsettle our routine thinking and present us with new possibilities and meaning in life.
- Those from the Devil (whose existence and role will be discussed in greater detail later) try to pass off what is harmful as attractive and lead us in the wrong direction.
- Those from within ourselves, he says, are thoughts and experiences that impressed us in the past.

To evaluate a choice he uses the example of a merchant examining a valuable coin to see if it is genuine or not.

- What is our first impression, does it seem genuine?
- Is it all that it promises to be (what it says on the label)?
- Does its weight feel right (is the reasoning on which it is based too light)?
- Has it been accepted by experts (the Elders and apostles)?

In this conference he introduces a more personal element, drawing on incidents he has seen or heard about. When a person cannot decide what should be done, despite their efforts to locate where the thought came from and to evaluate it with the four questions, they should humbly seek the advice of an Elder.

Moses's examples of how other monks went wrong illustrate the fact that no one is more deceived than when they are persuaded by themselves to despise the counsel of the Elders and rely on their own opinion and judgement.

Thus, humility means an acceptance of human limitations and the need for help from God and others. It can demand the surrender of one's personal opinion because, in theory at least, the Elder had greater wisdom and is closer to God. Without a sense of humility and gratitude, closeness to God and others was unthinkable.

Abba Moses admitted not all can be considered good counsellors just because of their age. This was a problem when the demand for unquestioning obedience became widespread in monasteries. Once the word of the abbot came to be seen as 'the will of God' it had to be accepted unconditionally even when it seemed unreasonable. The explanation was that it taught humility, 'the mother of all virtues'. Later Cassian will hear numerous stories of monks who underwent undeserved sufferings because of a misunderstanding or incompetent Elder.

An Irish practice that is said to go back to the early monastic period gave importance to having an 'Anam Cara', a soul friend, to whom one could go for advice and encouragement. Brigid of Kildare claimed, 'Anyone without a soul friend in life is a body without a head.' However, for John Cassian the monastic Elder was more than a 'compassionate presence'. He or she should not be slow to give positive direction and to reprove if necessary.

As illustrated by the story of Serapion, verbal confession of faults in front of others was another step in practising humility and making spiritual progress. Expressing one's regret in words was seen as taking the sting out of any damage done to the person themselves or to another. Later an opportunity was arranged each day for monks to come forward to admit their lapses before the assembled community. This developed into the sacrament of Penance, to which Irish monks made a contribution by introducing private, as opposed to public, confessions. It was an opportunity to discern the direction in which one's life was going and consult on what corrections were necessary.

Discernment may 'among all the virtues hold the supreme and first place', but humility is 'the mother of all virtues' and, as such, has priority.

CONFERENCE 3

The Way Forward

◇◇

Abba Paphnutius was a priest who had been in the desert of Scete for as long as people could remember. He was ninety when we visited him and he had lived in the same cell all that time, walking the five miles to church on Sundays. On his way back he carried a bucket of water on his shoulders, his supply for the week. By exemplary humility and obedience he overcame his weaknesses, and by avoiding company he enjoyed continuous meditation.

We were anxious to meet such a famous monk but approached his cell with trepidation. However, when he heard the story of our pilgrimage he accepted us warmly and agreed to talk with us. He began by praising our commitment. He noted that in our search for the truth we had given up our homeland, journeyed long distances, put up with the discomfort of the desert and shown willingness to imitate the practices of the monks we met.

We replied that we should not be praised for something we were still far from achieving. Such approval from a widely respected Elder might make us complacent, while what we needed was a lesson on how far we still had to go.

Paphnutius: Let us consider then what we are trying to do and the stages we must pass through. After that you can judge how far you have come. There are three ways in which we can feel called to a more spiritual life. The first is directly by God, the second is through the influence of others and the third is by a crisis in life.

A calling from God is when some inspiration takes possession of our heart and bids us follow God and keep his guidance. This is the way Abraham and blessed Anthony were called.

The second calling is when we are stirred to follow the example or words of a holy person as the people of Israel were by Moses. That is the way I myself felt called.

The third calling is when some crisis in our life drives us to look for God, just as the people of Israel turned to God in their distress.

Of the three, the first two may seem the highest, but even the third can lead to earnestness and perfection. In fact, some called in the first and second manner have gone cold after an eager start because they were not careful to bring the remainder of their life to a successful end. Judas is an example. On the other hand, one famous abbot reached perfection even though he had fled to the desert because of a murder he had committed. And then there is Paul, who persecuted Christians but later became a great apostle.

Once we have decided to respond to God's invitation we must pass through three stages or renunciations: making light of wealth, rejecting the inducements of the world and detaching our souls from all visible things so we can set our heart on what is invisible.

It would be no advantage to complete the first without going on to the second and then on to fixing our whole mental gaze on the things of God. In earnestly seeking things above and things of the spirit, the soul no longer feels that it is imprisoned in this fragile flesh and bodily form, but is caught up into such an ecstasy as not to hear words with the outward ear, or to busy itself with gazing on the form of things present. No one can understand what this is like if they have not tried it.

The first renunciation is of something that is not our own but the goods we got from God through another. We only own what we possess in our heart. Therefore this first renunciation does not on its own confer perfection.

If we advance to the second, we renounce something that really does belong to us, that is, our own weaknesses.

With the third renunciation we rise above all that is esteemed glorious in present-day society, and with heart and soul look down on what is subject to vanity and destined to pass away. Then we 'come into the land which I will show to you'.

From this we clearly see that as we hasten to the way of salvation through being stirred up by the inspiration of the Lord, so too it is under the guidance of his direction and illumination that we attain to the perfection of the highest bliss.

Germanus: Please tell us what place free will has to play in this. Are our efforts not also worthy of praise?

Paphnutius: We know that God creates opportunities of salvation in various ways; it is in our power to make use of the opportunities granted to us by heaven more or less earnestly. Abraham was obedient to the call of God to leave his own country.

However, even if we practise every virtue with unceasing efforts, with all our exertions and zeal we can never arrive at perfection on our own. No mere human diligence and toil of itself is sufficient to deserve to reach the splendid reward of bliss, unless we have secured it by means of the cooperation of the Lord and his directing our heart to what is right.

There are many examples of this in the Old Testament, and truly the saints have never said that it was by their own effort that they secured the way in which they advanced and gained perfection of virtue. Rather they prayed for it from the Lord, saying 'Direct me in the truth', and, 'Direct my way in thy sight'.

King David prayed that he might thoroughly understand. He knew that what came to him by nature would never be sufficient.

Take the example of the man who prayed, 'Lord, help my unbelief' (Mark 9:24). So thoroughly did those apostles and men in the gospel realise that everything that is good is brought to perfection by the aid of the Lord, and not imagine that they could preserve their faith unharmed by their own strength or free will, that they prayed that it might be helped or granted to them by the Lord.

The Lord said, 'Without me you can do nothing', so how foolish is it to attribute any good action to our own diligence and not to God's grace and assistance?

This plainly teaches us that the beginning of our good will is given to us by the inspiration of the Lord, when he draws us towards the way of salvation either by his own act, by the exhortation of another or by compulsion.

Think of the story of the ten lepers whom Jesus cured. Only one returned to thank him. God receives and commends those who are grateful but looks for and censures those who are thankless.

It is right for us to hold with unwavering faith that nothing whatever is done in this world without God. For we must acknowledge that everything is done either by his will or by his permission.

Germanus: Yet there are passages of scripture which say, 'If my people would have listened to me'; 'But my people would not hear my voice.' Do these not show that the decision to obey or not obey lay in the power of these people? How then can it be said that our salvation does not depend upon ourselves, if God himself has given us the power either to listen or not listen?

Paphnutius: We need to be careful not to make false interpretations. Note who speaks and who does not listen. Consider that just as the power of free will is evidenced by the disobedience of the people, so the daily oversight of God who declares and admonishes is also shown. God was with them all the time, telling them what was right but leaving them free to decide what to do.

* * *

At this point it was almost midnight. The discussion had been a long one with the Abba drawing examples and lessons from the Old and New Testament. As we prepared to leave the cell Paphnutius had a final word of advice. Some progress in the first renunciation (giving up worldly goods) and even in the second (overcoming weaknesses) might give the impression that we were already well on the way to perfection. However, we had not yet reached the stage at which we could even start to imagine the heights to which a monk can rise and the perfection which in so many ways exceeds what has been experienced up to now.

Suitably humbled, we retired to our sleeping place.

◇◇

Some who are drawn to exploring the spiritual side of life take up the challenge with a sense of being called directly by God. Not quite as dramatic as St Paul's Damascus experience, yet clear and personal.

Others are impressed by the example of good people they meet and want to know what inspires them. This can lead to trying to imitate them.

Still others are disillusioned by what they have experienced in life so far and decide they want something more durable and satisfying. This can spur them on to recognise and explore their spiritual side.

Paphnutius says that all three such beginnings can lead to the same lifelong commitment to searching for God. He himself began with the second; he was influenced by the life of others.

No matter what influenced the call, three basic 'renunciations' or discardings are needed to develop a 'pure heart', the fixing of one's whole mental gaze on God. Thoughts of wealth and comfort, ambitions for power and popularity, and attachment to visible things must be given up so the heart can see what the eye cannot see.

These three steps remain at the core of Christian spirituality. They will be mentioned and stressed again and again in the conferences.

Germanus's first concern echoed a question that rocked Western Christianity at the time. The gap between the creator God and his too human people was so great that without the initiative of an invitation from God, humans could never hope to rise above their mortal limitations. Did that mean that human intentions and efforts to seek God have no value on their own?

Two opposing sides were typified by contemporaries of Cassian, Augustine of Hippo and Pelagius the Celt. Augustine was deeply conscious of the immensity of God and the weakness of humans. Drawing on Romans 5:12–21 and 1 Corinthians 15:21–22, he was convinced that the disobedience of Adam and Eve (the Original Sin) had greatly weakened the free will of humans to the extent that they could do no good without the help of God. He assembled an impressive list of quotations from the Bible and early Church Fathers to prove his point.

Pelagius represented those who believed the Original Sin had weakened free will, but that humans were still capable of choosing between doing either good or evil. He too had an impressive list of authorities to support his argument.

Others joined in the debate, some going to the extreme of denying any power to free will and others denying any need for

God's help. The discussion was later taken up by Luther and Calvin, leading to a major division in the Church.

In responding to Germanus, Paphnutius did his best to find a balance between the two sides, but later both he and Cassian were accused of giving too much importance to an independent free will. Today their view is widely accepted.

This issue was important for the Desert Fathers and Mothers, because if human beings ultimately are not responsible for their actions there is no reason to try to improve oneself. This will be taken up again in Conferences 13 and 23.

It also brought up the practical question of whether sexual instincts can be controlled or not, and Germanus discusses this in Conferences 12 and 22.

The question of free will takes up much of the third conference and may seem a diversion from the topic of making spiritual progress. However, Cassian and Germanus needed the reassurance that their efforts would not be wasted and that they could face up to the challenge with confidence.

It could be said that Paphnutius's idea of a spiritual life is more suited to those in enclosed monasteries rather than to those struggling with the cares of everyday life. However, the expectations described by St Paul in 1 Corinthians 13 applied to all committed Christians. The 'three renunciations' prepare all travellers for that journey, though the manner and extent to which each responds will be determined by their ability and circumstances.

CONFERENCE 4

Working in Partnership

Our next meeting was with Abba Daniel. Abba Paphnutius had been so impressed by Daniel's humility, learning and sanctity that he had him ordained priest. He had hoped Daniel would succeed him as abbot but as it happened Daniel would predecease him.

With Abba Daniel we shared one of our concerns. Often in our cells we were filled with feelings of gladness and delight that surpassed words. Even in sleep, our petitions rose up powerfully to God. Yet at other times we felt weighed down with unreasonable depression. Our cells became intolerable, reading palled and our prayers wavered and became vague. We seemed unable to fix our gaze on God and our thoughts wandered off in other directions. What caused this wavering?

Daniel: The Elders offer three reasons for periods of spiritual dryness.

The first is carelessness. This is when, through our own fault, we let ourselves become lazy, allowing thoughts to grow in our minds which act like thorns and thistles, depriving us of the fruits of meditation.

The next is when, while actually trying to do what is right, we allow the Devil to find his way into our hearts and draw our hearts away from their good intentions.

The third is the presence of temptations allowed by the Lord. God permits them for one of two reasons. Either to humble us by reminding us of our weaknesses and dependence on his help or to test our perseverance and remind us of the need for effort, for we are generally more careless about keeping whatever we think can easily be replaced.

We must remember that God's grace and mercy are always active; without them our efforts would be useless. They inspire even the careless and indifferent with spiritual thoughts, rouse the slumberers, enlighten those blinded by ignorance and reprove and chasten us that we might be stirred by compunction.

When we are filled by God's sudden visitation the soul is ravished with delight and caught up, as it were, into an ecstasy of spirit so that it becomes oblivious of the fact that it is still in the flesh. However, at other times a seeming absence of God, such as mentioned by you, can be to our advantage. It helps us to recognise our own weakness and tests our love. We have a contest, as it were, implanted in our bodies by the action and arrangement of the Lord.

Germanus: We are beginning to understand what you are saying, but could you please explain further? There seem to be three struggles: the flesh against the spirit, the desires of the spirit against the flesh, and thirdly, the free will in the middle, having to decide whether to follow the flesh or the spirit.

Daniel: Let us then examine what we mean by the flesh, the spirit and free will.

The word 'flesh' is used in scripture in many ways. Sometimes it stands for the whole person, body and soul. Sometimes it stands for bodily weaknesses and desires. Sometime it stands for actual sins. Sometimes it stands for relationship as, 'We are thy bone and thy flesh'.

We must distinguish which 'flesh' we are discussing here. Obviously it is not in the sense of 'the Word was made flesh', or 'all flesh shall see the salvation of God'. When we speak of the flesh we mean body-based desires, as opposed to the spiritual desires of the soul.

Since the two exist within the one person there is bound to be tension.

The flesh delights in dissipation and sensuality while the spirit does not dwell on passing desires. The one wants to have plenty of sleep and to be satiated with food; the other is nourished with vigils and fasting so as to be unwilling even to admit to sleep and food for the needful purposes of life. The one longs to be enriched with plenty of everything, the other is satisfied even without the possession of a daily supply of bread. The one seeks to look sleek by means of baths and to be surrounded every day by crowds of flatterers, the other delights in dirt and filth and the solitude of inaccessible desert and dreads the approach of mortals. The one lives on popular esteem and applause, the other glories in injuries offered to it and in persecutions.

It might seem strange that God would create humans who need both body and soul to flourish yet for the two to be in perpetual conflict. They have free will to decide which gets priority, but free will itself is easily compromised if it seeks to please both parties. It tries to restrain the emotions but not to cause any suffering, to promote chastity without limiting instincts and to be humble without loss of worldly honour.

If left on our own to decide between two conflicting needs, we can prefer the easier road. Lukewarmness, not perfection, will be the result. We know from experience that spiritual progress is achieved only by constant effort and humility of spirit. We control the flesh by restraint, acquire purpose of heart by reading and prayer, preserve patience by endurance, serve our master and follow after the truth amid the opposition of the world.

Yet the two sides of human nature do need each other. The spirit does not allow the mind to be dragged into unbridged license; neither does the weakness of the flesh allow the spirit to be drawn to unreasonable aspiration after holiness.

Thus the struggle between body and spirit has its advantages. Bodily reluctance to take on strict disciplines prevents the over-zealous from doing damage to themselves, while the prick of conscience can make a person think twice before doing some wrong they had planned. The devils were not so lucky because, as spirits, what they decided to do was implemented immediately! No salutary second thoughts came in to amend their wicked intentions!

From this we can gather that the struggle that arises in us between flesh and spirit is not to be feared and can actually be extremely useful to us.

Germanus: Could you tell us in similar simple terms what is the difference between the carnal man and the natural man, and is the natural man worse than the carnal?

Daniel: According to scripture there are three kinds of soul. The first is carnal, the second natural and the third spiritual.

'Carnal' souls are those who know something about God, the gospels and the Spirit but are still too immersed in worldly interests to fully appreciate them and implement the demands of faith in their daily life.

'Natural' souls are those are those who know nothing about God and may even regard religion as foolish.

'Spiritual' souls are those in whom the word of God has come alive and who are actively engaged in seeking perfection.

As monks, we begin by renouncing the world of the 'carnal'. However, we should not think that because of this renunciation we are well on the way to perfection. To think that would lead us to carelessness and indifference; we could settle for pride in having rejected the world and make no further progress in spiritual growth. Those who are lukewarm are actually worse off than those who are 'carnal' or 'natural'. The 'carnal' and 'natural' can more easily be brought to a state of spiritual awareness than a monk who has set out on the road towards perfection but has lost his fervour and humility.

I have often seen cold and worldly heathens attain spiritual warmness, while monks who were lukewarm were unable to do so.

Indeed, I feel ashamed of how many turn out who said they wanted to renounce the world. They put on monks' robes but didn't like to change their old practices. They gathered wealth with the excuse that they needed to support their relatives or to start a new congregation of which they would be abbot.

Some put on an appearance of seriousness and gravity, others rejoice in relaxing the rules and talk freely on matters that are unsuitable and foolish. The cases are numerous. There are those who have given up great wealth but have not got rid of their former greed. If they become too careful about mats, baskets, blankets, books and other trifles, the same passion holds them as before. They actually guard and defend their rights over them so jealously as to get angry with their brethren because of them.

What difference does it make whether one gives way to covetousness in the matter of large and splendid things or in the matter of merest trifles? Indeed, we may think a man to be far worse if he has made light of great things and then becomes a slave to little things.

The renunciation of riches does not lead to perfection of heart if it claims to embrace poverty but still keeps the mind of wealth.

◇◇

The two spiritual learners have run into a very human and inevitable difficulty. At times they enjoy a reassuring and energising experience of God's closeness but then stray thoughts enter their minds and they are back in a troubled world. Achieving constant awareness of God's presence seems to be beyond their human capability.

Abba Daniel offers them three possibilities for their sudden dryness and lack of energy. It can be because of a lack of effort on their part, temptations of the Devil or a jolt from God rousing them to renew their efforts.

The struggle within ourselves is caused by the tensions between our bodily driven desires ('the flesh') and our spiritual hope ('the soul'). Sometimes body-based emotions can be so strong that they override our best intentions. It is as if someone, a tempter, is actually beside us, forcing us to do something we know we should avoid.

Such reminders of our weaknesses prevent us from becoming too self-reliant and proud. They can also inspire us to renew our efforts and to be more careful.

Germanus wants to know more about this inner struggle between 'the flesh' and 'the soul'.

Daniel explains that the 'flesh', or body, is what keeps a person alive and ensures they can live a full life. The 'soul' is what calls the person beyond bodily necessities to the ultimate goal in life. It is not strange that the two have different priorities. In fact, we need both of them. One enables us to survive and keeps us reminded of our human limitations. The other prevents 'the flesh' from getting too caught up in its immediate concerns.

In this inter-play Daniel sees 'free will' as an independent judge between the two, but inclined to favour 'the body' unless guided by careful discernment.

Finally, Daniel makes a telling distinction between three kinds of people. There are those who have some knowledge of religion but are too caught up in their daily affairs to be concerned about developing their faith (the 'carnal'). There are also those who have no experience of or interest in religion (the 'natural'), and, finally, there are those who actively seek to deepen their faith (the 'spiritual').

A person can move from one category to another during their life and, he warns, those who consider themselves 'spiritual' may not be so in practice. To suffer from lack of concentration in prayer was not unusual and no disgrace. How they dealt with the challenge was what mattered.

CONFERENCE 5

Eight Dangers Ahead

We had heard about Abba Serapion from Abba Moses and were anxious to meet him. He had become a highly regarded member of the Assembly of Elders and was noted for his discretion.

From the discussion with Abba Daniel we very aware of our shortcomings. We wanted Abba Serapion to explain the origin and cause of our faults and how they could be overcome.

Serapion: There are eight principal faults to which everyone is prone. They are: gluttony, fornication, avarice, anger, dejection, acedia (lethargy), boasting and pride.

These faults can be divided into two types: bodily, such as gluttony, and mental, such as covetousness. They can affect us in any of four ways. Some, such as gluttony and fornication, need the body to function, while others, such as pride and vainglory, are in the mind only. Some are aroused by what is outside the body, such as covetousness and anger, while others, like acedia and dejection, are initiated by internal feelings.

There is no shortage of biblical examples. Even Jesus, in the desert, was tempted by gluttony, vainglory and pride, the three sins of Adam and Eve in the garden.

The first six of the eight weaknesses are connected with each other in as much as gluttony is likely to lead to fornication, and fornication to covetousness and so on. As a result they should be dealt with in the same way; having overcome one we must immediately turn our attention to the next. In order to overcome acedia (lethargy), we must first overcome dejection, and to get rid of dejection, anger must be dealt with, and so on.

The final two weaknesses, vainglory and pride, are different. When the other six have been eradicated they spring up like weeds.

When it comes to dealing with these weaknesses, each person must begin by discovering their own greatest fault and direct all their efforts to getting rid of it. It is like the challenge facing hunters in a dangerous forest. They direct their first assault against whatever beast they see to be the strongest and fiercest, and when they have despatched the strongest beasts, then they can more easily lay low the remaining ones which are not so terrible and powerful.

In managing our main weakness, we should pray with special anxiety and fervour, asking that we may be more especially on our guard against it and so succeed in gaining a speedy victory. We cannot possibly overcome such mighty foes by our own strength unless supported by the aid of God. Each day we refer the whole of our victory over our weaknesses to God himself.

We can compare ourselves to those who have fallen into the clutches of many creditors. They can pay off all but one and that one comes to bother them every day.

Germanus: In scripture Moses reckoned that the people of Israel were opposed by seven nations and tradition has assigned a major fault to each of them. Yet you say the number of major faults or sins is eight. How is this so?

Serapion: Everyone agrees there are eight principal faults that affect a monk. In Deuteronomy Moses was speaking about the period after God's people had left Egypt, the most powerful and dangerous nation.

There they had many dangers to overcome. For us the greatest and most threatening weakness is gluttony and when we overcome it we still have to face seven other temptations, which brings the number to eight.

Take the example in scripture of the man from whom an unclean spirit was cast out, only for the spirit to return and, finding the house clean and tidy, invite seven worse spirits to come and join him. So the man's last state was worse than his first.

Those seven spirits were said to be worse because gluttony would not in itself be so harmful if it did not open the door to the other passions – fornication, covetousness, anger, dejection and pride – which are clearly hurtful to the soul in themselves.

Each of the faults has its own special corner in the heart, a recess which it claims for itself and from which it never ceases to oppose the contemplation of holy and heavenly things.

As for remedies, no one can hope to gain perfect purity of heart by means of abstinence alone. We fast because when the flesh is brought low by that means we can with greater ease enter the struggle against our other faults.

Neither are our battles all fought in the same order because, as we mentioned, attacks are not always made on us in the same manner. We begin each battle with due regard to the character of the attack being made on us so that while one person will have to battle against the fault that stands third in the list, another will engage the fourth or fifth.

* * *

And so did Abba Serapion discourse to us on the nature of the eight principal faults, and so clearly did he expound the different sort of passions that are latent within us – the origin and connection of which, though we were daily tormented by them, we could never before thoroughly understand and perceive – that we seemed almost to see them spread out before our eyes as in a mirror.

◇◇

On examining their bodily driven desires ('the flesh'), as opposed to their spiritual nature ('the soul'), the early monks distinguished eight basic weaknesses to which all human shortcomings could be traced. They are the feelings or instincts that can monopolise our heart and prevent it from seeing God.

The earliest list is attributed to one of Cassian's teachers, Evagrius Ponticus. Cassian calls the weaknesses the 'Eight Principal Faults'; they were later reduced to seven. They are gluttony, fornication, avarice, anger, dejection, acedia (lethargy), boasting and pride

The eight, or seven, became a checklist for anyone trying to understand their inner conflicts and how to manage them. In *The Institutes*, Cassian devotes a lengthy chapter to each, indicating that all of them are of equal importance. He describes their characteristics and how they are interrelated.

These human weaknesses are to be avoided not just for the damage they cause to the individual and to society, but because of the disruption they cause in one's relationship with God. The Irish monk Columbanus prayed, 'May no one and no thing separate us from the love of Christ ... that we may abide in him here.'

Some may be surprised that the first 'fault', and the one given most attention, relates to food. Cassian and other writers of that time saw gluttony as the initial shortcoming to be overcome as it was the source of all the other failings.

Examples given of 'gluttony', or letting food play too great a role in one's life, include snacking outside meal time, consuming beyond what is healthy and becoming attached to luxurious foods (one of the English translations for 'gluttony' is 'gourmandising'). Fasting was an obvious antidote.

However, Cassian also urged moderation in fasting and insisted that only in a healthy body could a healthy spirit thrive. Monks could enjoy their simple meals (and they were simple), but food, or any other pleasure, should not dominate one's identity. 'A person is the slave of the one by whom they are conquered' (2 Peter 2:19).

Cassian compared himself and other spiritual seekers to athletes preparing for the Olympic Games, with which they were very familiar. Anyone wanting to achieve a goal in life, whether in sport, art, academic studies or politics, must be prepared to give up other interests, unhealthy diets, time-consuming hobbies and a social life. This applies equally to those on a spiritual journey. Once a person is clear about their destination everything else takes second place to getting there.

The first step for beginners, then, is to overcome limitations set by their body. One means of training the appetite is fasting. It became a common practice in monasteries and soon spread beyond their walls, especially during Advent and Lent. The purpose is to develop restraint and self-control.

The second most dangerous fault is 'fornication', or lack of sexual restraint. For the monks, this is less a reminder of the physical restrictions set by the sixth and ninth commandments than the controlling thoughts that might distract them from their primary obligation. This is the context in which sexual matters are discussed in more detail in Conferences 12 and 22.

The other six weaknesses (avarice, anger, dejection, weariness, boasting and pride) also get a chapter each in Cassian's *Institutes*. All eight were seen as related to each other and having to be attended to in turn. Dealing with them called for genuine humility, a recognition that we need support from others, both human and divine.

The 'eight' were revised by Pope Gregory in 590, and their number was reduced to seven. They then became familiarly known as the Seven Deadly Sins or Seven Capital Sins.

A parallel list of Seven Heavenly Virtues was promoted in the Middle Ages but did not attract the same interest.

Germanus brings up an argument from scripture, concerning Israel and the seven nations with whom it fought, interpreting this in an allegorical sense. Conferences 12 and 18 will describe the various ways by which scholars at that time found different levels of meaning in the Bible.

CONFERENCE 6

The Good, the Bad and the Indifferent

When we heard the news of a massacre of monks in Palestine, our thoughts turned to the implications of this tragic event.

The monks had lived near the village of Tekoa for many years, gaining a reputation for holiness and perfection of life. Suddenly they were attacked and killed by a group of nomads. Since the holy men were held in such high regard people were rushing to recover their bodies and even fought for possession of their relics.

At that time we were visiting Abba Theodore, a man famous for his common sense who lived at Cellae, eighty miles across the desert from Scete.

Our question to Theodore was: Why did God allow so great a crime to be committed against his servants?

Theodore: Such questions often exercise the minds of those who have not much faith or knowledge. They imagine that the prizes and rewards of the saints are bestowed in the short space of this mortal life.

We should not fall into the same shallow thinking. In this world God does not reward good men with good things, and evil men with evil things.

We ought to know in the first place what is really good, and what is bad, so that when we grasp the true meaning of the scriptures, and not the false popular ones, we shall escape being deceived by the errors of unbelievers.

What is the good, the bad and the indifferent?

The only real good in humans is what leads us to sincere faith in things divine and adherence to the unchanging good.

We should not call anything bad except sin alone, which separates us from the goodness of God.

Indifferent things can be good or bad according to the mind or wish of their owner: riches, power, honour, bodily strength, beauty, life itself, death and poverty. Riches are good if shared with the needy but bad if amassed for a life of luxury and not used to meet the needs of the poor.

Therefore those who enjoy the greatest riches, honours and powers of this world should not be deemed to have secured what is best, but only something indifferent. The good person who uses them well is afforded opportunities to do praiseworthy works and bear fruits that will endure, while those who abuse their wealth have little place in God's plan; they risk sin and death.

So, does God ever allow evil to be forced on his saints, either by himself or someone else? You will certainly find that this never happens. The only evil is sin alone, which separates us from God, and no one can be forced to do evil if they do not consent.

Germanus: Yet we often read in holy scripture that God has created evil or brought it upon men, as in the passage, 'There is none besides me. I am the Lord and there is none else: I form the light and create darkness, I make peace and create evil' (Isaiah 45:6,7).

Theodore: The word 'evil' here is better understood as 'afflictions'. These are often seen as 'evil' by those on whom they are brought but it can be for their own good. Just as a doctor has sometimes to inflict pain on those he wants to cure, the sorrows and losses that some have to suffer can turn out to be a blessing.

When the Lord said, 'Lo, I will bring evils upon them' (Jeremiah 11:11), he wished to bring the people to a point where they would realise their mistake and hasten back to him in whom their prosperity lay.

Those things that are brought upon us as evil by our enemies, or by any other people, should not be counted as evil but as things indifferent. The evil we consider ourselves to be suffering is in fact indifferent. For in the end it will not be what the person who brought them upon us thinks in his rage and fury, but what we who endured them make of them.

And so, when death has been brought upon a saint, we ought not to think that an evil has happened to them but a thing indifferent. It is evil to a wicked person, while to the good it is eternal rest and freedom from evil.

Germanus: Well, then, if a good man does not suffer any evil by being killed, but actually gains a reward for his suffering, how can we accuse the man who has done him this good by killing him?

Theodore: We have been talking about the act itself, not the intention of the person who performed it. The wicked person should not go unpunished just because he was unable to, in fact, harm a good man. The endurance and goodness of the victim are of no profit to the perpetrator but only to him who patiently endured what was inflicted on him.

Take, for example, the Devil, who did not gain from testing the patience of Job, and the fate of Judas who helped bring about the death of Jesus.

We must develop our left hand as well as our right, making us spiritually 'ambidextrous'. By this I mean that while we make good and proper use of fortunate events, on the other hand we should equally be able to benefit from unfortunate events.

Our right hand develops spiritual abilities, overcomes desires and passions, longs more intensely for the future, feeds on spiritual contemplation and pours forth prayers to God with greater purity and readiness.

When a monk is troubled by temptations, inflamed with desires, on fire with emotions or puffed up with pride, he knows that he is attacked 'on the left hand'.

Those not puffed up by pride in the achievements of the 'right hand', and who struggle manfully against those on the left, can use both hands as 'right hands' and carry off the prize of victory on the left hand as well as the right.

Think of Job, the just man who tried to use his resources well but also had to put up with many sufferings and temptations. He said, 'If we have received good at the hand of the Lord, should we not also receive evil? Naked I came out of my mother's womb and naked I shall return thither. The Lord gave and the Lord hath taken away, as it hath pleased the Lord, so is it done; blessed be the name of the Lord.'

Though we can be tested in both prosperity and adversity, we are afflicted for three different reasons: to test us, for our improvement and because we deserve it.

Abraham, Job and the people of Israel in the desert were tested to prove themselves.

For the sake of improvement it is said in the Apocalypse, 'Those whom I love, I reprove and chasten.'

The Lord threatened the people of Israel with plagues as punishment for their sins (Deuteronomy 32:24).

There is also a fourth reason. Some sufferings are brought upon us simply for the manifestation of the glory of God and his works. As it says in the Gospel, 'Neither did this man sin nor his parents, but that the works of God might be manifested in him' (John 9:3).

There are many other examples in scripture of God's intervention in people's lives, which they accepted in faith, and they remained steadfast despite every kind of trial. A person should not be like wax, whose shape is easily changed, but like hard steel that can leave a mark on others while upon itself nothing that happens can leave a mark.

Germanus: How can our mind constantly preserve this faith unaltered and always continue in the same state?

Theodore: The mind cannot possibly remain in the same state; if it is not moving forward it will fall back. Only God is unchangeable. We should always, with incessant care and anxiety, give ourselves up to the acquisition of virtue and constantly occupy ourselves with the practice of it lest, if we cease to go forward, the result should immediately be a going back.

We ought always to remain shut up in our cell. If we leave and then come back it will be difficult to regain that fixed purpose of mind that we had attained through much effort. We will also have missed out on the advance we could have made if we had stayed.

God alone is unchangeable and good as his goodness is not the result of effort but a natural possession and so he cannot be anything but good. No virtue then can be acquired by man without the possibility of change. In order that when, once gained, that virtue may be preserved it must be watched over with the same care and diligence with which it was acquired.

A change for the worst does not come from a sudden slip. As Solomon said, 'Water dripping drives a man out of the house on a stormy day' (Proverbs 27:15). If the roof has been neglected, a drip starts when it rains, the rafters decay and the house collapses. So, slowly and gradually, the passions can take over the soul.

* * *

We were delighted with this 'spiritual repast'. The mental pleasure with which we were filled by this conference outweighed the sorrow that we had experienced before from the death of the saints. For not only were we instructed in things about which we had been puzzled, but we also learned from the raising of that question some things that our understanding had been too small for us to ask about.

◇◇

In the year 823 Norse pirates raided the Skelligs and wiped out the whole community. It was a repeat of the incident at Tekoa some 400 years earlier and probably raised the same questions: Why did God allow such holy men to suffer so dreadfully? Similar questions are still being asked today when atrocities occur.

Abba Theodore replied that questions like those are the sort that trouble the minds of people who have not much faith or knowledge. God's thinking is beyond our comprehension, but the little we know of it indicates that it is much wider and deeper than ours. Today, when people visit the Skelligs they are likely to question the sanity of the monks who lived in such harsh conditions, but Theodore and his companions knew why time in such 'cells' was necessary to make sure one's faith in God's goodness would never falter.

Theodore explained by answering three questions: What is good and what is evil? Why do misfortunes happen to people who deserve to be rewarded? Why is our trust in God's goodness so fragile that we can easily come to doubt it?

The only real good is that which leads us to deepen our faith and seek what lasts. The only real evil is sin, which separates us from the goodness of God. Everything else is 'indifferent'.

Riches, power, honour, bodily strength, beauty and life itself are indifferent: good if shared with the needy but bad if amassed for a life of luxury. What makes them good or bad depends on the intention of their owner. The good person uses the opportunity to do praiseworthy works and bear fruits which shall endure, while those who misuse their wealth have little place in God's plan.

Since the only evil is that which separates us from God, no one can be forced to do evil if they do not consent. God never allows evil to be forced on his saints.

As to Germanus's insistence that scripture speaks of occasions when God brought evil upon people, Theodore replies that there the word 'evil' is better understood as 'afflictions'. We can be afflicted for three different reasons: to test us, for our improvement and because we deserve it. God may also have another reason altogether, as it says in the Gospel, 'Neither did this man sin nor his parents, but that the works of God might be manifested in him' (John 9:3).

We should be prepared to accept what is good as well as what seems bad because both can benefit us. In a manner of speaking, we need to develop our left hand as well as our right. We must make good use of fortunate events and, on the other hand, be equally capable of benefitting from unfortunate events.

Why are our faith and our thinking so vulnerable to doubts? It is because the human mind never remains in the same state; if it is not moving forward it is falling back. Only God is unchangeable. To train our mind we should stay shut up in our cell. If we leave and then come back we will find it hard to return to the level we were at before and will have missed out on the advances we could have made in the meantime.

Preserving one's faith in the face of contradictions and setbacks remains the challenge for everyone on a spiritual journey. Accepting that God's plans and priorities are different from ours may seem fatalistic, but fatalism provides no meaning or value in living. People of faith are called to discover the positive and the good in life.

CONFERENCE 7

Inner Whisper or Outer Prompt?

◇◇

It was Lent when we got to visit Abba Serenus, whose name indicates peace of mind. His chastity was so advanced that, it was said, he was never disturbed by natural impulses even when asleep.

As usual we were questioned on our reasons for coming to see him, what we had learnt in the desert and how we were progressing.

We answered that we were now more aware of what we should be striving for, but at times the challenge involved seemed beyond our strength. We were confused and ashamed because, especially in the area of keeping our thoughts chaste, achieving the ideal seemed beyond our ability.

We asked: what is the good of having learnt what is best if it cannot be attained even when it is known? Was it our own fault or was it because of a flaw in human nature that these wanderings of mind and body are found in humans?

Serenus: It is dangerous to jump to conclusions before discussing the matter with others and examining it from various aspects. If a man, ignorant of swimming, insisted that the solid body could not be supported by water and would drown in it, you would not quickly agree with him. It might be his experience but his opinion is still not true.

The mind is ever shifting. That is its nature. It must by its own fickleness wander about and stray over all kinds of things until it finds what it is looking for. If it is possible to discover what we are looking for by prudence and industry but we fail to do so, we ought to blame our own laziness and carelessness, not our human nature. It is in our power to ascend or descend, to improve or fall back, otherwise we could not be held to account.

Take the example of the centurion in the Gospel (Matthew 8:9) who drew on his own experience of his own strengths and limitations. We too can become 'centurions' in the spiritual contest.

We will find out that we can and ought to cling to the Lord if we are to have our wills disciplined and the desires of this world cut off. We should not to be wearied by these wanderings of the mind or relax our fervour, or be drawn away from watchfulness through a dangerous despair. No virtue is acquired without effort and no one can attain to that mental stability which he desires without great sorrow of heart.

Germanus: Perhaps the tendency of the mind to roam might be checked if we did not have such a great swarm of tempters around it, ceaselessly urging it to do what it has no wish for. Weak people like ourselves would not expect to be able to withstand such pressure if we had not been encouraged by words like yours.

Serenus: There are such external powers but all they can do is incite, they cannot force anyone to do wrong. Just as they have such power to incite, so we have the power to reject or submit. When we are afraid of their power and assaults, we may also claim the protection and assistance of God.

Germanus: What is the power of spirits and their relationship to us? Can they talk to us and incite us? They seem so close that we can have difficulty, without God's help, distinguishing what comes from them and what is from our own free will.

Serenus: There is a real relationship between us as both we and they are created of the same substance. However, no spirit can possess another spirit; only the deity has that prerogative.

Germanus: We see people possessed by evil spirits acting and speaking under their influence. If the person and the spirit are not united how is it the person's words and deeds are no longer their own but the demon's?

Serenus: Some people are completely taken over and don't know what they say or do. Others know and can remember. But that is not because the evil spirit penetrates into the actual substance of the soul, and being as it were united to it, uttering words and sayings through the mouth of the sufferer. The person has not lost their soul but has become weak. The unclean spirit overwhelms their soul and interferes with its intellectual powers, just as wine or a fever can affect the functions of the body. The Devil was told, 'Lo, I give him [Job] into your hands, only preserve his soul' (Job 2:6). That is, do not smother the ruling power of his heart with your weight.

Germanus: How can we say that spirits are unable to influence our thoughts? For example, it says in scripture, 'The Devil had put it into the heart of Simon Iscariot to betray the Lord' (John 13:2).

Serenus: No one doubts that spirits can influence our thoughts but they do it from outside and not from within. The thoughts they suggest are based on indications of where our interest lies. For example, when we look anxiously at the sun to see if it is near mealtime they know there may be feelings of greed. It is the same when there are suggestions of sexual desire, grief, anger or rage. They build on those indications. Even we ourselves can know the thoughts of others from their expressions.

Some spirits seem to focus on a certain weakness and specialise in exploiting it.

Germanus: Should we then believe that there is an order and plan in the attacks of these spirits?

Serenus: Usually it is difficult for the wicked to work together in harmony but there could be times when they work in unison. Sometimes, when one has been defeated, another will emerge to continue the fight in his place.

The weaker spirits engage with beginners and those easily influenced, while the stronger spirits focus on those who are more advanced in spiritual growth. However, God does not let us be tempted beyond our strength.

The struggle is like a battle in which both sides must exert their strength and in which both sides can experience the joys of victory or the despair of defeat.

That evil spirits do not have the power to hurt humans is shown in the story of Job. Even young men could not survive the rigours of the desert if spirits had unlimited power to hurt and tempt them.

If you listen to stories about the first monks in the deserts, it seems that then the struggle with spirits was more intense and demanding. It got to the stage when one man would have to stay awake all night to repel their sudden attacks. Now the attacks do not seem to be so intense. That may be because the strength of the spirts is weaker as the light of the gospel spreads in the deserts, or else our carelessness has made them relax their first onslaught and replace open attacks by using coaxing methods to get monks out of their cells to wander around and get into difficulties. There was a saying, 'Eat and drink and sleep as much as you like, but stay in your cell!'

It is clear that unclean spirits cannot make their way into the bodies of those they are going to attack in any other way than by first taking possession of their minds and thoughts. Once they have robbed them of fear and the recollection of God and spiritual meditation, they take up their dwelling in them as if possession was given over to them.

Such people may seem outwardly unaffected by the spirits, but inside they are entangled in unworthy cravings. They are spiritually dangerously ill but they are not aware of it. We know that the fall of some saintly men began with a minor fault. Even small imperfections can prevent achievement in the spiritual journey.

Learning from scripture, there are two reasons why we ought not to hate or despise those who seem to be delivered up to various temptations or to the spirits of evil. First, none of them can be tempted without God's permission, and second, all things that are brought upon us by God, whether they seem to us at the present time to be sad or joyful, are inflicted for our advantage as by a most kind father and compassionate physician.

Germanus: Why then do we see such people scorned and shunned by everybody and actually kept away from Holy Communion?

Serenus: If we really believed that all things were brought about by God for the good of souls we would never despise them. As for forbidding them Holy Communion, I cannot remember such a practice. Indeed, such victims were encouraged to receive Communion daily if possible, as it is a safeguard for soul and body.

Those whom we should consider wretched and miserable are individuals steeped in sin but showing no visible signs of the Devil's possessing them.

There are sinners who seem to pass through this world without any humiliation, even rejoicing in great riches, and this led the prophet to ask, 'Why does the way of the wicked prosper? Why is it well with all of those who transgress and do wickedly?' (Jeremiah 12:1). The Lord's response was to direct doctors and physicians to heal them.

The scriptures are full of descriptions of the various sorts of evil spirits and their favourite approaches. It would take too long to draw up a list.

Germanus: I do not doubt the various grades of evil spirits but where do the differences among them come from? Were they created in some way to serve wickedness?

Serenus: This brings up some wide and deep questions but it is already night and there is no time to deal with them properly. Let us take up the discussion again tomorrow, and if the Holy Spirit grants us a prosperous breeze to penetrate more freely into the intricacies of the questions raised, we could continue to discuss with redoubled delight what the Lord may have given us for our common improvement.

◇◇

According to Serenus, even in his day awareness of the existence of evil spirits was weakening. Anthony, the first hermit, was famous for his fights with demons and there were stories from the early days that in monastic communities one monk would stay awake all night in case they were attacked. Serenus ventured that consciousness of such spirits had lessened as the light of the gospel spread in the deserts, or perhaps the demons saw new opportunities in the growing laxity of the monks for trying indirect methods to get them to leave their cells.

Since that time serious belief in spirits or devils has become less clear-cut, though even in the Western world traces can be found in Halloween celebrations, horror films and superheroes. In Asia and Africa the belief remains strong and Western missionaries have had their scepticism and presumption tested when brought face to face with a request to expel evil spirits from a possessed person.

That the desert monks had a keen awareness of demons is to be expected. They were following the path of Jesus who began his public life by spending forty days in the desert, where he was tempted by the Devil. In this discussion on why the mind wanders during prayer, demons were seen as tempters. Conference 8 will take up a wider discussion on evil spirits.

Serenus's clarifications on spirits as tempters include the following:

- Evil spirits can only entice or tempt, they cannot force a person to do something against their will.
- They cannot take over a person completely. They can possess the body but not the soul. Their influence is similar to that of alcohol, which can affect a person's emotions and movements.
- They build on what they find in people. If the person shows greed or a tendency towards anger and pride they will use those entry points and gradually take over.
- They have no coordinated plan, but one takes over from another when resistance has been lowered.
- Once a person forgets God and their spiritual task, the demons can begin to invade their mind and take over.
- Some people may continue to live good lives and appear unaffected, but inwardly they have already been changed.
- Do not be quick to judge people who seem possessed by evil spirits and don't prevent them from receiving the Eucharist. It is a safeguard and medicine for the soul given by God, 'the compassionate physician'.

Modern authors have admired Cassian's ability to explore the psychology of temptation and a reading of the full text of this conference will explain why.

While official Church teaching still accepts the existence and influence of spirits, both good and evil, modern theologians are more guarded. However, anyone believing there are more things in heaven and on earth than we can fully understand cannot but accept the possibility. As Serenus explains, just because we think something is impossible does not mean it is impossible: a person ignorant of swimming may insist that the solid body cannot be supported by water and would drown in it. That might be their opinion but it still is not true.

Cassian himself was wary of talking about demons. His teacher, Evagrius Ponticus, said, 'I cannot write about all the villainies of the demons and I feel ashamed to speak about them at length or in detail for fear of harming the more simple-minded among my readers.'

CONFERENCE 8

Real and Imaginary

The next evening, after we had completed our duties and returned from the church, we went to Abba Serenus's cell, where he treated us to a most sumptuous repast.

Instead of his usual frugal meal, the Abba mixed boiled herbs and poured over them a little more oil than usual. Then, he set before us table salt and three olives each, after which he produced a basket containing parched vetches from which we each took five grains, two prunes and a fig apiece. The custom of pouring a few drops of oil on the food, just enough to taste, was a local practice to make a show of eating well and removing any temptation to take pride in eating an oil-less meal.

When we had finished Serenus said, 'Let me hear your question, the consideration of which we postponed till the present time.'

Germanus: What is the origin of the great variety of hostile powers mentioned in scripture (Ephesians 6:12 and Romans 8:38)? Where did all that enmity and malice come from?

Serenus: Some parts of scripture are very clear and can be understood easily by almost everyone. However, in other parts the meaning is so concealed and involved in mysteries that care and skill are needed when discussing and explaining them.

The scriptures are a rich and fertile field that produces foods, some of which are easy for humans to consume and others that have to be cooked to make them edible. Similarly, parts of scripture are easy to understand and can be taken literally, while others need to be watered down by an allegorical interpretation.

We can boldly state our own opinion of the passages whose meaning is clearly explained. But those passages that the Holy Spirit has inserted in Holy Scripture with veiled meaning need to be carefully considered and brought together so they can be discussed or argued in an orderly manner. When a difference of opinion is expressed, it can be considered reasonable and held without injury if found not to be opposed to the faith.

The question we are discussing has not been widely debated and the answer is not obvious so we will consider it in the light of scriptural proofs and the tradition of the Fathers, not mere personal opinion and conjecture.

First, we agree that God never created anything that is substantially evil. To believe that would be to slander God as the creator and author of evil, of having formed utterly evil wills and natures.

It is also accepted that before God created humans he brought celestial spirits into being and that some of them, through pride, lost their heavenly status. In the scriptures we find mention of their various ranks, which may come from the heavenly rank they previously held or are just titles they gave themselves.

Spirits exist and inhabit the space between heaven and earth. Fortunately divine providence has made them invisible. If humans could see them they would live in daily dread or quickly come under their influence. Also, to encourage us we are told that we have two angels, one good and one bad, clinging to each of us.

References to activities and powers of the evil spirits can be found in scripture. One monk I know, in the middle of the night witnessed a gathering of demons at which their leader received reports from countless spirits, praising those who were successful in tempting humans and rebuking those who were not.

Germanus: There are two questions that puzzle me: What did it mean in Genesis (6:4) when it says that 'fallen angels had intercourse with the daughters of men'? And who is the Devil's father in the phrase 'for he is a liar and his father' (John 8:44)?

Serenus: You have propounded two not unimportant questions to which I will reply to the best of my ability in the order in which you have raised them.

We cannot possibly believe that spiritual existences can have carnal intercourse with women. Scripture relates how, after Cain killed the righteous Abel, Adam had another son, Seth. He was another upright man and his descendants followed the path of justice and goodness. They were called 'angels of God' and 'sons of God'.

The descendants of Cain were evil and a law forbade the family of Seth from marrying any of Cain's descendants lest they be contaminated. However, the daughters of Cain were very beautiful and Seth's sons, 'the angels of God', could not resist marrying them. Thus, the scriptural passage quoted.

Germanus: If there was no formal rule at that time prohibiting them from intermarrying, how could they be considered guilty?

Serenus: When God created humans he implanted in them complete knowledge of the law (that is, what is right and wrong), and if it had been observed there would not have been any need for another law to be given. But when human freedom was corrupted and the opportunities for sinning became common, the law of Moses was added to strengthen the original law. 'The law is not made for the righteous, but for the unrighteous and insubordinate, for the ungodly and sinners, for the wicked and profane' (1 Timothy 1:9).

As for the passage, 'He is a liar and his father', as we said a little while ago, spirit does not beget spirit, just as soul cannot procreate soul. When the Devil became puffed up with pride and said in his heart, 'I will ascend above the height of the clouds, I will be like the Most High' (Isaiah 14:14), he became a liar and not only a liar but the father of all lies when he told humans, 'Ye shall be gods' (Genesis 3:5).

* * *

Dawn was approaching and the discussion, which had gone on for two nights, came to an end. This conference had drawn our barque from the deep sea of questions to a safe harbour of silence. As a result, a wider and boundless space had opened up, reaching out beyond the sight of our eye.

We saw that the fear and love of the Lord cannot fail and we prayed that we remain steadfast and wise in all things so we would be shielded unharmed from the darts of the Devil.

The words of this conference so fired us that when we went away from the old man's cell we longed with a keener ardour of soul than when we first came for the fulfilment of his teaching.

◇◇

Abba Serenus offers answers to Germanus's question about the origins of spirits but begins with a word of caution.

What we know about demons comes from the scriptures and other religious texts, but we have to be careful in our interpretation. While some parts of scripture are very clear and can be understood easily by almost everyone, the meaning of other parts is less obvious. Some passages are easy to understand and can be taken literally, while others need to be explored by an allegorical interpretation. In Conference 14 the various ways in which scripture can be understood are dealt with in more detail.

Serenus warns that the question they were discussing had not been widely debated and the answer was not obvious, so they should consider it in the light of scriptural proofs and the tradition of the Fathers, not their personal opinions and conjectures.

The reason for his warning was because many accounts drew on a Hebrew religious text, the Book of Enoch. It describes the origins of demons and giants and why some angels fell from heaven. It also relates how fallen angels took human wives. The book, written between 300 and 200 BC is not accepted as biblical revelation by Jews or Christians in the West, but was of considerable interest to scholars in Cassian's time and later, because of its unusual contents.

Serenus, in giving his personal opinion, repeats that God never created anything that was substantially evil. Angels were created before humans but some lost their heavenly status because of pride and were expelled from heaven by the Archangel Michael.

Spirits exist and are all around us but fortunately we cannot see them. Some are trying to lead us in the wrong direction and others guard us. Less common was Serenus's assertion that each person has a 'good angel' and a 'bad angel'. In this he was drawing from 'The Shepherd of Herman', an early second-century writing no longer recognised as part of the Bible.

Germanus's question about fallen angels and the daughters of men show how the Enoch tradition is retained in the Bible. Serenus has no trouble in explaining them.

Today the interest in angels continues with TV programmes, movies and wellness classes, fuelling a demand for books, posters and cards linked with them. The Charismatic Movement has also brought about serious discussion about the place of spirits. Devil-related plots continue to be popular in literature.

With the Skelligs' location on the western Irish seaboard and nothing but wild seas and darkness beyond, the monks had every reason to take this conference seriously. In 950 a church was built there, dedicated to Michael the Archangel. From then on the rock was known as Skellig Michael. It protected the country from the spirits Michael had once expelled from heaven. Similar monuments can be found on other coasts of western Europe, including Mont St Michel off the coast of Normandy, St Michael's Mount in Cornwall and St Michael's Abbey on the border between France and Italy.

CONFERENCE 9

Releasing the Feather

Our visit with Abba Isaac, a disciple of Anthony, the 'Father of all monks', was an opportunity to return to what we considered our greatest challenge – how to live constantly in the presence of God through prayer and contemplation.

Isaac: The aim of every monk and the perfection of his heart incline him to continual and unbroken perseverance in prayer and, as far as it is allowed by human frailty, it strives to acquire an immovable tranquillity of mind and a perpetual purity of spirit.

These lofty heights of perfection cannot be reached unless a clearance of human faults be first undertaken and the decayed and dead rubbish of the passions dug up. Then the strong foundations of simplicity and humility can be laid on the solid and living soil of our breast, or rather, on the rock of the Gospel.

All concern for temporal matters must first be got rid of entirely. We must leave aside not only business concerns but all backbiting, vain and incessant chattering, anger and moroseness, as well as lust and covetousness. When this has been done, a deep foundation of simplicity and humility must be laid down that can support a tower that reaches to the sky.

This tower should become a spiritual structure housing all the virtues, where the soul is kept free from all conversations and roving thoughts so it can be raised up little by little to the contemplation of God and spiritual insight.

As a starting point we should be aware that what we think about before we start praying will influence how we pray. It can make us angry or gloomy, recall our former desires or some foolish joke or go back to a previous conversation. Therefore, if we do not want anything to haunt us while we are praying, we should be careful before our prayers to exclude such thoughts from the shrine of our heart that we might pray without ceasing.

The nature of the soul has been compared to a very fine feather which, if not weighed down by moisture or any other weight, is naturally borne aloft by the lightness of its nature. So our soul, if not weighed down by the cares of this world or damage done to it, will be borne aloft to the heights by the light breath of spiritual meditation, leaving low things behind.

We should take note of the ways in which the Lord points out how the soul is weighed down. He did not mention adultery, or fornication, or murder or blasphemy or rapine, which everyone knows to be deadly and damnable, but excessive eating and drinking and the cares or anxieties of this world (Luke 21:34).

The last three weigh down the soul and separate it from God, but it should be very easy for us who are cut off from visible cares to avoid drunkenness and excess. Yet there is a spiritual drunkenness that is more difficult to avoid and a care and anxiety for this world which often ensnares us, even after our renunciation of all earthly goods. As the prophet says, 'Awake, ye that are drunk but not with wine' (Joel 1:5).

The Elders have laid down that anything that goes beyond the necessities of daily food and unavoidable needs of the flesh, belongs to worldly cares and anxieties. For example, when a job bringing in a penny would satisfy the needs of our body, we try to extend it by longer toil in order to get two pence or three pence. Or when a covering of two tunics would be enough for our use both by day and by night, we manage to become the owner of three or four. Or when a hut containing one or two cells would be sufficient, but in the pride of worldly ambition and greatness we build four or five cells, splendidly decorated, and larger than our needs require. In such ways we show the passion for worldly lusts whenever we can.

For other people such activities might seem trivial and of no consequence, but for the monk they are dangerous. They prevent him from laying aside earthly limitations and aspiring to God alone on whom his attention should ever be fixed. For the monk, even a slight separation from the highest good must be regarded as present death and most dangerous destruction. Only when he is free can he pray without ceasing.

Germanus: If only we could hold on to spiritual thoughts in the same way and with the same ease with which we conceive them! They vanish only too soon and what we have experienced does not seem to have any permanent effect on us. It is hard to pray without interruption.

Isaac: It is quite clear we cannot always offer up the same type of prayer all the time. Depending on the state of the soul each moment of prayer will be different. A person prays one way when happy and another when weighed down by sadness and despair, one way when enjoying spiritual progress and another when oppressed by numerous distractions ...

The apostle taught us four types of prayer: 'I exhort therefore first of all that supplications, prayers, intercessions and thanksgivings be made' (1 Timothy 2:1). We will examine these four individually and then consider whether they should be included in every prayer, offered in turn or offered by those who have most experience in them.

'Supplications' are implorings or petitions concerning sins, in which one who is sorry for his present or past deeds asks for pardon.

'Prayers' are those by which we offer or vow something to God ... We pray when we renounce this world and promise that, being dead to all worldly actions and the life of this world, we will serve the Lord with full purpose of heart.

'Intercessions' are what we are wont to offer up for others, making requests either for those dear to us or for the peace of the whole world.

'Thanksgiving' is what the mind in ineffable transport offers up to God, either when it recalls God's p benefits or when it contemplates his present ones, or when it looks forward to those great ones in the future which God has laid up for those who love him.

The first seem appropriate for beginners, the second for those who have already attained some progress in the quest for virtue, the third for those who have completed their vows by their works and the fourth for those who have torn from their hearts the guilty thorns of conscience and are now free to contemplate with pure mind.

However, the mind that is advancing to the perfect state of purity will take in all these at one and the same time. This offers up to God inexpressible prayer of the purest force, in which the Spirit itself, intervening with groanings that cannot be uttered and that we ourselves cannot understand, pours forth to God supplications so great that they cannot be uttered by the mouth nor even at any other time be recollected by the mind.

Yet those who remain under the punishment of terror and fear of judgement are so smitten with sorrow that they can be filled with no less keenness of spirit than the one who, through purity of heart, gazes on and considers the blessing of God and is overcome with ineffable joy and delight.

The kind of prayer we are aiming at should pour forth from the contemplation of the good things to come or from the fervour of love. In this way, little by little, our mind is raised through the regular course of those intercessions.

The New Testament shows us how Jesus used the four types of supplication. Let us take up the Lord's Prayer and examine each section in turn.

The first is 'Our Father who art in heaven, hallowed be thy name'. This expresses our familiar relationship with God, our hope to be where he is, and asks that our efforts and good works help to increase reverence for his holy name.

'Thy kingdom come' expresses a wish that the kingdom of God comes soon, either in the hearts of those now seeking it or as the reward for all those who do God's will.

'Thy will be done on earth as it is in heaven' asks that, just as God's will is carried out by the angels in heaven, we too can imitate their example in this world.

In the phrase, 'Give us this day our daily bread', one evangelist uses the word 'super-substantial' instead of 'daily'. The former emphasises its grandeur and holiness while the latter intimates the purpose of its use and value. 'Daily' also indicates that without it we cannot live a spiritual life for a single day; yesterday's supply is not enough.

'Forgive us our debts as we forgive others' gives us an opportunity to moderate the sentence for any crime we may have committed.

'Lead us not into temptation' does not mean we ask never to be tempted; temptations improve our power of endurance. Rather we pray that we are not overcome by the temptations that come our way.

'But deliver us from evil' pleads that we are not tempted by the Devil beyond what we are able to endure.

In the Lord's Prayer, there are no petitions for riches, honour, power or bodily health. For the author of eternity would have men ask of him nothing uncertain, nothing paltry and nothing temporal.

The Lord's Prayer, based on the words of Jesus himself, would seem to contain all the fullness of perfection. However, it can also lead us on to a still higher stage, which is known and tried by very few but transcends all human thought. It pours forth richly, as from a copious fountain, in an accumulation of thoughts, expressing in the shortest possible space of time such great things that when the mind returns to its usual condition it cannot easily utter or relate. This is the prayer that Jesus, when he retired alone to the mountain, is said to have poured forth in silence.

Who is able, with whatever experience they have been given, to give a full description of the varieties, reasons and grounds of the convictions that lead one to pray?

Our spirit may be stirred by a verse of the psalms we recite, the harmonious singing of a brother or the reverence of the chanter; also the exhortations of a holy person at a spiritual conference that stirred our emotions. The death of a brother or someone dear to us can have the same effect. Even regretting our past coldness and carelessness can lead to a fervent spirit of prayer.

There is also a variety of ways in which these emotions and convictions express themselves. It can break out in shouts of uncontrollable joy that may be heard in a neighbouring cell. It can also be in complete silence, the amazement of a sudden illumination that quietens all words as the overawed spirit keeps its feelings to itself or pours them out in groanings that cannot be uttered.

Germanus: I have at times shed tears of joy at the Lord's presence when I put my weaknesses before him. There is nothing as sublime as that state of mind. However, when I want to recreate that experience at another time, I cannot do it, no matter how many tears I shed.

Isaac: The shedding of tears and experience of God's presence are not caused by just one feeling. Sometimes it is because our conscience is stirred by a realisation of our faults, or when we contemplate the future glories that await us. It may be fear of the consequences of our own sins or the hardness of heart in others.

These tears are not those squeezed out from dry eyes when the heart is hard, though even then they are not worthless as they show our good intentions. However, such laborious efforts will never attain the richness of spontaneous tears. Forced tears may even distract supplicants from steadfastly fixing their attention on spiritual progress.

There is something I learnt from the blessed Anthony. He was so persistent in prayer himself that he was disappointed to see the sun rising since it brought his time of prayer to an end. He taught us that a perfect prayer is never one in which the monk understands himself and the words with which he prays.

If we pray with confidence, then, and feel that by pouring out our prayer we have obtained what we are asking for, we can have no doubt that our prayer was effective. As it is said, 'Whatever you ask when you pray, believe that you shall receive it, and it shall come to you' (Mark 11:24).

Germanus: What about us who have no accumulated merit on which we can draw and who still experience the lure of temptations?

Isaac: Scripture tells us that there are certain times when our prayer will be heard, no matter who we are or what we have done. Such is the case when two or three pray together, when there is dogged persistence, when prayer is accompanied by works of mercy and a felt need for God's help. There is never a reason for despair when the request is salutary and eternal. The Lord encourages us to keep urging him so we should never slacken once we begin.

We should also observe the advice to pray in our cell with the door closed. We do this when we remove from our hearts all thoughts and anxieties, make our prayers in secret and in close contact with the Lord.

Finally, we should pray often but briefly. If we try to pray for long periods some idle thought might be implanted in our heart and lead us astray.

***

Once more the approach of night brought the discussion to an end, but we felt we had only touched the surface of a very deep subject. We agreed to meet again in the early morning. Although we believed we had learnt something of the nature of prayer we still needed to discover how to persevere in it, how progress might be made and how that progress might be maintained.

Abba Isaac states, 'The goal of every monk and the perfection of his heart leads him to constant and uninterrupted perseverance in prayer.' How can this demanding task be achieved? Prayer is a 'lifting of the mind and heart to God'. To be constant, must this be practised consciously every moment of the day or at regular intervals or at designated times? These are the questions Cassian and Germanus keep asking. In this, the first of two conferences on prayer, Abba Isaac concentrates on the basics: how to prepare for prayer, the different types, the highest form, the example of the Lord's Prayer and the effectiveness of prayers. He will deal with the question of constant prayer in Conference 10.

These are two chapters or conferences that deserve to be read in their entirety. They are classics of Christian spirituality and still recommended as essential reading for anyone entering a monastery or commencing spiritual training.

Before beginning to pray, the mind and heart must be cleared of unnecessary distractions. The 'three renunciations' have already been mentioned in Conference 3 as the initial stages in spiritual growth. Progress or lack of it in those areas will influence our state of mind as we prepare to pray. If we are feeling angry, sad, lightheaded or anxious, those moods will persist in occupying our thoughts and hold us back.

There are different types of prayer and we do not have to use the same form all the time. Depending on our needs and state of mind at the time our approach can be adjusted.

Isaac quotes St Paul to identify four types of prayer. Later scholars would consider the interpretation as forced and too intent on a literal interpreting of the great saint, but it does illustrate the essential functions that prayers fulfil. Isaac also indicates how progress can be made.

The Lord's Prayer is based on the words of Jesus himself and considered the model for Christian prayer. Isaac elaborates on each phrase and notes that it does not include any petitions for riches, power or health.

Finally, he assures his listeners that if we pray with confidence and ask for what it truly beneficial, our prayer will be granted.

All prayer should lead us progressively to a stage when we no longer need to use reason, study, reflection or imagination to be in contact with the divine. This is the highest stage to which everyone is called and it should be a normal development in the deepening of faith. Isaac describes the fulfilment as silent prayer in its purest force, so great that it cannot be uttered by the mouth nor at any other time be recollected by the mind.

There will be more on this in the next conference. Perhaps unexpectedly, Isaac ends by saying we should pray often but briefly.

CONFERENCE 10

Holding the Focus

Before our discussion on prayer could continue, the annual pastoral letter from the Bishop of Alexandria arrived with a warning against a heresy based on a literal interpretation of Genesis 1:27: 'So God created humankind in his image, in the image of God he created them; male and female he created them'. It maintained that if humans were created in the image of God, all the attributes, emotions and needs found in humans are to be found in God too, since humans are the mirror image of God.

This idea was widely shared in the desert communities and many monks found it hard to accept the bishop's letter, which condemned this way of thinking as a throwback to the worship of idols with human features.

We were at Abba Paphnutius's community at the time. When Paphnutius asked a deacon named Photius to explain the contents of the letter to the monks he clarified that the 'image and likeness of God' in which humans were created was spiritual and not bodily. God can neither be apprehended by the eye nor conceived by the mind, so does not possess a body like that of humans.

We ourselves were disturbed by the violent reaction of one old monk. He cried out in despair, 'Alas, wretched man that I am! They have taken away my God from me! Now I have none to lay hold of. I do not know whom I should worship or address.'

We wondered how he could have such erroneous beliefs despite his many years of exemplary life in the desert and expressed our surprise to Isaac.

Isaac: We should not be surprised, as the monk is a simple man who has never received any instruction on the nature of God. He is still influenced by the old pagan devotion to gods in human form. The pure condition of prayer that we were discussing yesterday is not connected with any physical figure or image of the Godhead.

Our mind can be both raised and moulded if it forsakes considerations of earthly and material things and sees Jesus with the inner eye of the soul, either in his humility and in the flesh or as glorified and coming in his glory.

Jesus can be seen by those who dwell in towns, villages and hamlets – anywhere, that is, where people are occupied in practical affairs and work, but not with the same brightness with which he appeared to Peter, James and John. Jesus retired into the mountain to pray alone, thus teaching us that if we too wish to approach God with a pure and spotless affection of heart, we should also retire from all disturbances and confusion of crowds.

This will lead to the stage when every love, every desire, every effort, every thought of ours, everything we breathe, will be God. Then that unity that the Father has with the Son and that the Son has with the Father will be carried over into our understanding and our mind. Just as he loves us with a pure and unfeigned and indissoluble love, we may be joined to him with a lasting and inseparable affection.

The goal of the solitary should be to possess, even in the body, an image of future bliss, that they may begin in this world to have a foretaste of that celestial life and glory.

Germanus: You have increased the enthusiasm and interest you inspired in us by yesterday's discussion and we are fired with the desire for perfect bliss. We hope that you will be able to show us some method or way of keeping the idea of God always in our minds, so that even if our thoughts wander for a moment they could quickly recover and return to awareness of his presence.

Isaac: The clarity and shrewdness of your questions indicates that you are well on the way to purity of heart. Therefore I have no hesitation in introducing you to the entry point of what you are seeking.

To help those who seek to live continually in the presence of God, the earliest monks have passed on a prayer for repetition. It is, 'Oh God, make speed to save me, Oh Lord make haste to help me.' The formula was chosen from scripture because it embraces all the feelings that can be implanted in human nature and can be adapted to every situation.

It is humble, watchful, aware of weakness and confident of help. At moments of frailty or over-confidence it returns us to what is essential.

You should write this formula on the threshold and door of your mouth, you should place it on the walls of your house and in the recesses of your heart so that when you fall on your knees in prayer it may be your chant as you kneel, and when you rise up to go forth on the necessary businesses of life, it may be your constant prayer.

If you follow this practice you can achieve the first beatitude of the gospel, 'Blessed are the poor in spirit for theirs is the kingdom of heaven.' You can become a 'spiritual hedgehog', as it says in the scriptures, 'And the hedgehogs are a feeble folk, who have made their homes in the rocks' (Proverbs 30:26). What is feebler than a Christian, or a monk, who is not only not permitted any vengeance for wrongs done to him but is actually not allowed to suffer even a slight and silent feeling of irritation to spring up within?

Whoever advances from this condition will take in to themselves all the thoughts of the Psalms and have the scriptures opened for them with greater clearness. There will be no need to gaze on sacred images or use any words or utterances.

With purpose of mind all on fire, an ecstasy of heart will be ignited by some unaccountable keenness of spirit, and the mind will pour itself forth to God with groanings and sighs that cannot find human expression.

Germanus: You have described for us not only the method we were looking for but perfection itself. However, we would like one more thing explained. How can we keep a firm hold on this verse so it might always give us a steady grasp on spiritual matters?

I myself find that my studies jump from one subject to another. I seem unable to reject or keep hold of anything or to finish anything by fully considering and examining it. I am becoming only a toucher or taster of spiritual meanings, not an author or possessor of them.

Isaac: We have already spoken at length about these matters, but since it continues to concern you I will repeat the essentials for steadiness of heart.

There are three things that keep a heart steady: watching, meditation and prayer. But first, all cares and anxieties of this present life must be got rid of by persistence in work dedicated, not to covetousness, but to the sacred needs of the monastery. Pray without ceasing.

They pray too little who pray only at the time they bend their knees. But they never pray, even on their bended knees, who are distracted by all kinds of wandering thoughts. What we would like to be when we pray, that we ought to be before the time of prayer. The mind cannot help being affected by its previous condition. While it is praying it will be either transported to things heavenly or dragged down to earthy things by those thoughts in which it had lingered before prayer.

* * *

In reflecting on these discussions with Abba Isaac, we agree that we admired and wished to follow very closely the method the Abba had taught us. It seemed to us a short and easy way to perfection. However, we were to discover it to be an even harder system to follow than the one that had allowed us to wander here and there through the whole body of the scriptures without being tied by any chains of perseverance.

No one is ever excluded from perfection of heart because of illiteracy, nor is simplicity an obstacle in attaining purity of heart and soul. These lie close to all if only they will, by constant meditation on the verse he gave us, keep the thoughts of the mind safe and sound towards God.

◇◇

This conference begins with the reaction of some monks to an episcopal letter condemning devotions and prayers directed to a physical image of God in human form. It leads Isaac to discuss further the manner of encountering God directly and how to live constantly in God's presence.

Jesus can be found by all, whether they live in towns, villages or hamlets and are occupied in practical affairs or work. However, living constantly in God's presence and encountering him directly call for times of silence in our lives. There we can possess, even in the body, a foretaste of the future life. A stage will come when every love, every desire, every effort, every thought of ours, everything we breathe, will be God.

However, since the mind wanders constantly, is it humanly possible to give God uninterrupted attention?

Isaac provides an answer that has had enduring influence in Christian circles over the centuries. He recommends a quotation from Psalm 70, 'Oh God, make speed to save me, Oh Lord, make haste to help me.' Another translation is, 'Oh God, come to our aid. Oh Lord, make haste to help us.' That formula was chosen from scripture by the Elders because it embraces all the feelings that can be implanted in human nature and it can be adapted to every situation.

It can be used to bring the mind back to prayer when distracted or to maintain a high level of prayer and awareness. It can be repeated while doing any kind of work or performing some service. 'Let it send you to your knees as you rise from bed, let it bring you from there to every work and activity and let it accompany you at all times.'

The underlying message is that prayers activated by thinking, imagining and reflecting can bring us into the presence of God, but if we want to approach closer we must rely on the unconscious resources of the soul.

The method recommended by Isaac, repeating the invocation, 'Oh God, make speed to save ... ', was taken up by St Benedict, who instructed his monks to repeat it at least seven times a day and use it as the introductory verse for the recitation of psalms known as the Office.

The monks on the Skelligs had a chapel in which they could pray together as a community. Two chapters of the *Institutes* give detailed instructions on the number of psalms recited and related customs. During the major gatherings at morning and evening twelve psalms were recited and a section from both Old and New Testaments were read. Shorter sessions at terce, sext and none (third, sixth and ninth hours) were marked by three psalms. In this way, combined with private prayer at work and alone in their cells, the monks prayed 'without ceasing'.

In modern times John Main, inspired by John Cassian, founded the Christian Meditation Movement to enable anyone anywhere to join in the desert tradition. Verses such as that from Psalm 70 are used as mantra in twice-daily periods to develop a constant relationship with God. A similar approach can be found in the Centring Prayer, Lectio Divina and Brother Lawrence's 'The Practice of the Presence of God'. The methods differ but the goal is the same.

Short prayers and blessings as a reminder of God's presence became common in Celtic countries. An example is St Patrick's Breastplate: 'Christ be with me, Christ be beside me, Christ before me, Christ behind me ... '

Today the Angelus bell is an invitation to silence in towns and villages, and the tradition of families offering morning prayers, night prayers and the Rosary together were the beginning of a learning process for many.

CONFERENCE 11

The Three Motivations

For our next visit we were helped by the holy man Archebius, who had been carried by the local people out from the desert, where he had spent thirty-seven years, and made bishop of Panephysis.

Once Archebius was assured of our genuineness he proposed that we meet with monks who lived not far from his monastery. He spoke with enthusiasm of those holy men, whose length of service is shown by their bent bodies. Their holiness shines forth in their appearance so that the mere sight of them gives a great lesson to those who see them.

The bishop took up his staff and script, as was the custom, and acted as our guide. There were three monks he suggested we visit: Chaeremon, Nestros and Joseph. Chaeremon, over a hundred years old and unable to walk upright any longer, was the first we met.

As was the custom, we asked Abba Chaeremon for 'a word of guidance', and he replied that the infirmity of his body had made him relax the strictness of his life and destroyed his confidence in speaking. A teacher has no authority if he does not actually live out what he teaches.

We replied that the remoteness of the area and the solitude in which he lived should be enough to teach us everything we need to know but would he please lay aside his silence for a while and in a simple manner explain to us the principles of the goodness that we could see in him.

Chaeremon: There are three ways by which people are restrained from doing what is wrong and all of them can lead to fulfilment. These are the fear of hell, hope for the kingdom of heaven and the love of virtue. They reflect the three virtues of faith, hope and love.

Even though the three seem to aim at one and the same end, they differ in their degree of excellence. The first two belong properly to those who seek good but have not yet acquired the love of virtue. The third belongs to God and to those who have received into themselves the image and likeness of God. For only he does what is good, who is moved not by fear or by hope of reward but by a disposition for the good alone.

From the first step progress can be made to the higher path of hope. There we look for the promised reward but cannot attain to the love of a son who trusts in his father's kindness and liberality and has no doubts that all that his father has is his. The story of the prodigal son illustrates this.

We can only ascend to that true perfection when, as he first loved us for the grace of nothing but our salvation, we also love him for the sake of nothing but his own love alone.

There is a great difference between those who put out the fire of sin within themselves for fear of hell or hope for future reward and those who keep hold of the virtue of purity of heart from the feeling of divine love.

If we rely on the help of God and not on our own efforts we can pass from being a fearful servant or a hopeful mercenary to being an adopted child, with no sense of fear or greed. For how can a weak and fragile human nature be like God except in always showing a calm love in its heart and doing good for the love of goodness itself?

This sense of compassion will lead to a feeling of regret for the offences of others and remove any rigid judgements or censures of others.

Germanus: Yet the scriptures challenge what you are saying with words like, 'Fear the Lord, all ye his saints, for they that fear him lack nothing' (Psalm 34:9) and, 'I have inclined my heart to do righteous acts for ever, for the reward' (Psalm 119:112).

Chaeremon: Scripture summons different people to different grades of perfection; no uniform crown of perfection is promised to all. We read, 'There is no fear in love but perfect love casts out fear' (1 John 4:18). We are called by God from higher things to still higher in such a way that he who has become blessed and perfect in the fear of God can go from strength to strength, and from one perfection to another, till in the end is reached the still more blessed state, which is love. There the 'good and faithful servant' will join in the companionship of adopted children.

The first two reasons, fear of punishment and hope of reward, are not of no value. They are useful and introduce those who pursue them to the beginnings of blessedness. As the scripture says, in his Father's house there are many mansions.

There is a sublime fear that belongs to love, the fear brought about by earnest affection towards a father, towards a brother or sister, a friend, wife or husband. It is not dread, but care lest the warmth of this love should cool in even the very slightest degree towards its object.

There are then two fears. One is for beginners, for those still subject to the yoke and to servile terror, a penal fear. The other is the fear belonging to the perfection of which the God-man gave us a pattern and example. As scripture says, 'And the spirit of the fear of the Lord shall fill him' (Isaiah 11:2). This is not a passing fear but a spirit that possesses a person because it is closely joined to that love that 'never fails'.

Germanus: You have spoken to us about the love of God with great simplicity. Could you speak to us with equal freedom about chastity? We would like to know if can be achieved with any permanence. Can we reach a stage where there would be no more temptations or incitement to lust, and can we ever be free from carnal passion and the fire of excitement?

Chaeremon: Humans are indeed composed of both soul and body. However, before we begin to discuss matters of the body, which we can do shortly, it would be fitting to attend to one of the body's other needs – that of eating. Let us have some supper, and after it our minds might be more prepared to consider the matters you raise.

◇◇

If anyone came to the Skelligs with the expectation that doing penance for their misdeeds would help them escape punishment in the next life they would soon learn this was not the thinking of the community.

Chaeremon may have had such people in mind when he began the discussion with three reasons people stopped doing evil. One was fear of punishment, another was hope of a reward and the last was a striving to mirror the love of God. The first two could be useful starting points but the third was the goal of the Christian life.

He compares these three motivations to the fearful obedience of a slave, the selfish expectations of a servant or the attachment of a child to its parents. They can also be seen as expressions of faith, hope and charity. We fear because we believe in the formidable power of God, we hope for a promised reward but we seek to approach our creator Father out of love. As St Paul said, the greatest of these is charity, that is, love.

In passing from a servant's fear or a mercenary's hope to a child's freedom from terror and greed we can rely on the help of God.

This ascent to true perfection is possible only when we accept that God first loved us for what we are. Then we can begin to love God for the sake of nothing but God's own love alone.

In this way God calls us from higher things to still higher in such a way that we can go from strength to strength, and from one perfection to another, till in the end we reach the still more blessed state, which is love. It is achieved only by the person who does what is good, not out of fear or hope of reward, but by a disposition for the good alone.

This vision of Christian love, loving with no expectation of anything in return, is something that humans appreciate but find difficult to practise. It is what children might hope for from their parents, students from their teachers and the weak from those responsible for them.

The clarity of Chaeremon's description was stirring, but Germanus in particular was only too aware of human weaknesses. He had already expressed his concerns about the mind's tendency to wander, the almost overwhelming lure of temptations and human free will's difficulty in controlling strong instincts. Here he mentions chastity, which calls for more than refraining from sexual acts. The discussion so far has been about growing in the love of God, but that cannot exist without control of sexual distractions. Can we ever escape from the passions of the body as long we live in our mortal form?

Chaeremon considers this too important a topic to discuss hurriedly and puts it off to the next meeting. The implications of this question are explored in Conferences 12 and 22 and are a reminder that monks, too, were human beings, even if they were on the road to becoming 'saints'. In the Conferences, Cassian is not reluctant to give examples of everyday failings arising from the 'Eight Basic Weaknesses'. The *Institutes* lists these short-coming and directs how each should be dealt with. Whether the original motivation is fear or hope, it is enough to begin with, but has to be worked on to reach the ultimate goal, 'the blessed state, which is love'.

CONFERENCE 12

Brothers in Unity

We met again with Abba Chaeremon to continue the discussion with a focus on controlling sexual impulses.

Chaeremon: Germanus does well to put his question in the context of achieving the fullness of God's love. Perfect and perpetual chastity undoubtedly lead to such a goal.

The apostle Paul said, 'Put to death what is earthly in your life, that is: immorality, impurity, inordinate passions, wicked desires and greed' (Colossians 3:5).

The first thing the apostle mentions is immorality, which is related to bodily union. The second he calls impurity – thoughts that creep up on those who are sleeping or awake due to negligence. The third is lack of control or wantonness. The remainder are considered lesser sins: the desires of a weak will and avarice.

Those who have abandoned all for Christ give up not only their wealth but the desire for it. Similarly, those who have given up sexual activity should also give up the desire for it. If it were impossible to do this we would not be so instructed.

Experience has taught us that we cannot achieve purity of heart by fasts, vigils or study alone. Such practices are useful, but without God's help we would make little progress.

Just as a person can be on fire with a desire for money or with love for a beautiful woman, we too should see everything else as secondary as we seek God's love, praying ceaselessly for it. The desire for present things cannot be simply cut off. The mind's health cannot be preserved without retaining feelings of desire or fear, joy or sadness. Rather, we should plant spiritual pleasures within them and turn them to good use.

As a person progresses in mildness and patience, and keeps to the hard ways of the Lord, so also will they grow in purity of body. Until they acquire firm and perpetual peace they will be assailed by numerous attacks and will frequently repeat the verse, 'I have become wretched and am afflicted beyond measure' (Psalm 38:6–7). Our weakness is a reminder of our humanity and helps us grow in humility.

There are six achievements of chastity. The first is not to be overcome by sudden sexual impulses while awake. The second is not to dwell on coarse thoughts. The third is not to be moved by desire while looking at a woman. The fourth is not to permit movements of the flesh when awake. The fifth is not to be disturbed by thoughts evoked by reading or talking about human generation.

The sixth achievement is not to be deluded by indecent images even when dreaming. We do not believe such delusions are necessarily sinful, nonetheless they are an indication of a desire that is still deeply ingrained. Each person is tempted, even when asleep, according to how they behave and think while awake.

The highest degree of chastity has been experienced by only a few and, since it was granted to them by a personal grace, it is beyond description. No one can speak with authority on these matters except those who have gained knowledge of them through long experience and purity of heart.

As for bodily discharges during the night, those who have advanced in chastity know that what happened is merely part of the physical process by which nature operates.

Germanus: We know that it is possible for perpetual chastity to be preserved while we are awake through the grace of God and taking proper care. But we want to know whether we can also be free from this disturbance while we are asleep.

For two reasons we do not think it is possible. First, the mind is not alert enough to prevent it while no longer attentive. Second, when the bladder is full it arouses sexual instincts. If this does not lead to undesired pleasure, the lack of control at least humiliates us.

Chaeremon: You seem to have not yet grasped the meaning of true chastity. It cannot be maintained solely when awake through strict discipline. Integrity is not undermined by sleep. Chastity lives not by rigorous defence but by love itself and delight in its own state. It is not chastity but abstinence that is challenged by the appeal of adverse pleasure.

As long as we feel that we are being afflicted by disturbances of the flesh we can know that we have not yet arrived at the heights of chastity but are still trying to maintain abstinence. Perfect chastity is distinguished from abstinence by the sense of peace it brings. It does not fight with the movements of desire but passes over them with a feeling that can only be called holiness. When the body and the spirit start working together they provide mutual support as 'brothers in unity' (Psalm 133:1).

The more the mind has advanced to a more refined purity, the more sublimely it will see God. It will grow in wonder within itself rather than try to speak about it or find words to explain it. Whoever deserves to arrive at this state of virtue, after examining in the silence of their mind all the things that the Lord works in those who are his own by his special grace, will cry out, 'Wonderful are your works, and my soul knows them exceedingly' (Psalm 139:14). It is the wondrous work of God that a bodily human being, dwelling in flesh, would reject fleshly desires, would hold on to one state of mind in the midst of so many diversions and assaults and would remain changeless in every changing circumstance.

Once a holy man was jeered by a crowd in Alexandria. They mocked him, saying, 'What miracle will your Christ perform for you?' He replied, 'That I am not disturbed or offended by these or any greater insults that you might offer.'

Germanus: The wonderful vision you put before us seems beyond the capability of the ordinary person. Can you teach us how to achieve it and how long it will take? Knowing that would give us courage.

Chaeremon: It is difficult to determine how long it will take as each person's ability and circumstances are different. However, in general it can be said that it is possible to achieve this goal within six months for a person who has withdrawn from pointless conversations, can control their anger and concerns, is satisfied with just two meals a day, does not drink their fill of water and wake up after three or four hours' sleep, yet does not believe that these efforts alone are enough without the mercy and help of God. To realise that one cannot achieve this goal without God's help is a clear sign that true purity is near.

To summarise: Chastity is achieved when no wanton pleasure troubles the seeker when they are awake and no illusory dream leads them astray when they are asleep. When a disturbance creeps up on them during sleep due to the carelessness of a weary mind, do not be concerned. Just as it was aroused by no deliberate action, it returns to a calm state without any struggle.

This is what we learned from experienced teachers. It will probably be considered impossible by the lazy and negligent, but I am sure it will be accepted and approved by the earnest and spiritual. Since human beings differ from each other, the things to which their minds incline are dissimilar. As scripture says, 'Where your treasure is, there also will your heart be' (Matthew 6:21).

***

With these words Chaeremon ended the discussion and, as it was almost morning, he urged us, overwhelmed and anxious as we were, to avail of the remaining time to sleep. Otherwise our minds, wearied by the demands of the day, would lose their vitality and vigour.

◇◇

Germanus brought up a not uncommon concern: Is it humanly possible to fully control sexual instincts?

This conference and Conference 22 were omitted in early translations of Cassian's work because of the direct and explicit language used when discussing sexually related matters. It was feared that descriptions of male physiological concerns (not all included in these quotations) would be unsuitable for women and the young. Such unease was not evident in Cassian's time when body parts and sexual activity were discussed in a relaxed and open manner. It was not until the seventeenth century that sexual discussion was curbed and treated with delicacy.

Chaeremon praises the way Germanus framed his question. It was in the context of discussing the fullness of love for, and from, God. Perfect and perpetual chastity undoubtedly plays an important role in the relationship. The difficulty in achieving it cannot be ignored, but if chastity were not possible we would not have been encouraged to make the effort.

Chaeremon pointed out that those who have abandoned all for Christ give up not only their wealth but the desire for it. Similarly, those who have given up sexual activity should also give up the desire for it. However, the human desires we feel cannot be simply cut off; mental health cannot be preserved without retaining feelings of desire or fear, joy or sadness. We should plant spiritual pleasures within these and turn them to good use. In that way our minds will always seek higher things in which they can find pleasure and ignore temporal enticements.

Chastity, when achieved, is the state of being completely at peace in one's body with no contending instincts. It comes, not by repression, but by filling one's heart with a greater desire and love. The body and the spirit start working together, providing mutual support as 'brothers in unity' (Psalm 133:1).

Chaeremon believes that the task is not insurmountable, and if our emotions continue to be disturbed we should try to understand the roots of what is happening so we can overcome them. Our weakness is a reminder of our humanity and helps us grow in humility.

However, we should not confuse chastity with abstinence. The reason we abstain from unlawful sexual thoughts and actions is to preserve the peace of mind and feeling of closeness to God that chastity brings. It is abstinence that is challenged by conflicting feelings. As long as tensions continue we know that we have not yet arrived at the state of chastity but are still trying to maintain abstinence.

From his experience Chaeremon assures us that the highest degree of chastity has been experienced only by a few and no one can speak with authority on these matters except those who have gained knowledge of them over many years.

His conclusion is that chastity is achieved when no wanton pleasure troubles the seeker when they are awake and no illusory dream leads them astray when they are asleep. When a disturbance creeps up on them during sleep due to the carelessness of a weary mind, do not be concerned. Just as it was aroused by no deliberate action, it returns to a calm state without any struggle.

Germanus is not fully satisfied and will bring up his questions again in Conference 22.

Peter Brown, in *The Body and Society*, his study of early Christianity, sees Cassian asserting a different approach to sexuality from that of Augustine.

For Augustine, the disobedience of Adam and Eve had weakened the power of the free will to control human instincts, especially the strong sexual desires of concupiscence. The instincts now have a freedom of their own and will never again be completely controlled by will power. They are a reminder of humans' fallen state – only by God's intervention can a person be delivered from them.

Cassian, on the other hand, accepted sexual instincts as part of being human. There is no dualism. God created them for a purpose, to keep humans humble and prevent them becoming too pleased with themselves. They are also symptoms, and a warning, of other weaknesses still active in the unconscious – rage, pride and selfishness.

The Freudian tradition came to see sex as the basic instinct that influences other activities. Cassian saw it the opposite way. Excessive sexual desires revealed that unresolved instincts such as anger, greed and egotism remained in the psyche. Concupiscence was a symptom of what lay out of sight, hidden deeper in the identity than sexual desire. Like a doctor diagnosing a patient, the monk could measure the presence within of those de-energising flaws by the strength of his own sexual temptations. Concupiscence could, and should, be eliminated completely, but this can be achieved only when the other weaknesses have been dealt with. Then inner peace will finally come.

For Cassian, chastity depends not only on assistance from God but also on utilising the interdependence of body and soul. The body is a reminder of the limitations of the soul, just as the soul reminds the body that there is more to life than the eye can see. They must work together.

The Christian belief that the body will rise again along with the soul brought a new dimension to their relationship. The invitation of Christ embraces them both.

CONFERENCE 13

Liberty or Dependency?

After a short sleep we returned for the morning service and waited for Abba Chaeremon.

We were still thinking over the previous night's discussion. It would seem that an individual might strive with all their might but could never master themselves unless they acquired what they wanted by the gift of God. The holy man saw there was something serious on our minds and cut short the service of prayers and psalms to ask us what was the matter.

Germanus: Last night we heard that chastity is possible but it demands earnest effort as well as the grace of God. A farmer puts great labour into producing crops and gets credit for his hard work. Why then do we not ascribe the fruits of chastity to the efforts put into achieving it?

Chaeremon: Your example also shows that the efforts of the worker can do nothing without God's aid. Good crops are not just the result of hard work, they need rain at the right time and a calm winter. All the tedious labours of the farmer are no good without the Lord's assistance through nature. Human pride should not put itself on the same level as the grace of God and fancy that its own efforts are the cause of divine bounty. It is divine compassion that supplies the means for the completion of efforts.

It is God who initiates not only our actions but also the good thoughts that inspire us. From him we get the will to begin and the opportunity to carry out what we rightly desire. It is then up to us to humbly follow day by day the grace of God which is drawing us, and not to resist with 'a stiff neck'.

Germanus: But does that not destroy free will? Many non-Christians show remarkable virtue, even chastity. They know nothing of the scriptures nor do they believe in God, so are they not gaining chastity by their own efforts?

Chaeremon: I am pleased to see your eagerness to learn but surprised at your question. Yesterday you went as far as to suggest that purity of heart and chastity were so difficult to achieve that they could not possibly, even by God's grace, be bestowed on any mortal. Now you are suggesting that such a state could be achieved by heathens with their own strength. However, I understand that you raise this point only in a search for deeper understanding.

We must not think that those philosophers attained chastity of soul, as we think of it. They practised a type of chastity by which they restrained themselves from sexual intercourse but did not seek an internal purity of mind. Desire and passion were not shut out from their hearts.

Who would willingly endure the squalor of the desert, the continuous thirst for water and sleeping for only four hours, if it was not with God's grace? The Lord must give us both the wish and the opportunity to attempt those things.

We must also remember that God does not desire any of his little ones to perish but wants all, not just some, to be saved.

When God sees in us even the smallest spark of good will, which he himself has stuck in our heart, he fans and fosters it with his breath.

A comparison can be made with a man who is inflamed with most ardent love for a woman. The more he is slighted and despised by her the more he entreats her. In his goodness God not only inspires us with holy desires but actually creates opportunities for good results and shows to those in error the direction of the way of salvation.

We can appreciate how all day long God stretches out his hand to even an unbelieving and gainsaying people to guide them on the true path, but it is more difficult for us to explain how the completion of our salvation is assigned to our own will.

Holy Scripture supports the freedom of the will where it says, 'Keep thy heart with all diligence' (Proverbs 4:23). There are many more examples.

It raises the question, does God have compassion on us because we have shown the beginnings of a good will, or does the beginning of a good will follow because God has had compassion on us?

There are those who have taken up one or other side with great energy and scholarship but have created more confusion than understanding. The grace of God and human free will may seem opposed to each other, but really they are in harmony. We need both alike. If we withdraw one of them from the human condition, we will have broken with the Church's established beliefs.

We should not hold that God made humans in such a manner that they can never be capable of doing good or bad, or that he has not granted them a free will.

The grace of God always cooperates with our will for its advantage by assisting, protecting and defending. Sometimes it looks for some effort of good will so as not to appear to be conferring a gift on someone who is asleep. It continues to be free when, in return for some small and trivial effort, it bestows with priceless bounty such glory of immortality and eternal bliss.

Because of the faith of the good thief on the cross the abode of paradise was promised to him as a free gift. When Jesus acclaimed the good centurion, saying, 'I have not found so great faith in Israel' (Matthew 8:10), there would have been no grounds for praise or merit if he had only praised what he himself had given.

There are numerous other examples that clearly show the ways in which God draws people to salvation, but God's 'judgements are inscrutable and his ways past finding out' (Romans 11:33).

The grace of God is not dispensed according to the desserts of each person, it is superabundant and overflows the narrow limits of man's lack of faith.

At times he gives what we desire for our good, while at others he puts into us the very beginnings of holy desire. He is called our sponsor and our refuge.

If anyone thinks that they can understand or discuss exhaustively the ways God operates for our salvation, he is in contention with scripture, which says God's ways cannot be scrutinised or searched out.

However, the Fathers have taught that in comparison with the magnitude of God's grace, the role played by free will is limited.

The first stage of the divine gift is to inflame the person with the desire for everything that is good, but in such a way that the choice of free will is open to either side.

The second is to enable the practice of virtue, but in such a way that the possibilities of the will are not destroyed.

The third is to preserve the goodness already acquired in such a way that liberty is neither surrendered nor experiences limited.

For the God of all must be seen to work in all, inciting, protecting and strengthening, but not taking away the freedom of will which he himself has given.

***

At the conclusion of the discussion we felt that what we had learnt was nourishment that would prevent us from being overcome by the exertions of a difficult journey.

◇◇

Here the discussion on the role of free will, begun in Conference 3, is taken up in greater detail. Cassian (and Chaeremon) are aware of Augustine's insistence on the inability of humans to do anything worthwhile without God's help. It led to the concept of predestination, that only those whom God chose can be saved. This would seem to remove any role or responsibility for the decision-making free will of individuals.

In response, people like Cassian questioned the belief that there is no room for personal conversion or decision-making. Would this not also make meaningless the efforts of those in the desert, in monasteries and in the wider world to raise themselves spiritually?

Chaeremon does his best to articulate a balance. Our intellectual capability comes up short when we try to penetrate the mind of God. Those who think they can explain how God operates in our lives are ignoring scripture, which says God's ways cannot be scrutinised.

Some have taken up one or other side of the discussion with great intensity and created more confusion than understanding. The grace of God and human free will are not opposed to each other, they are in harmony. We need both.

It was a frustrating debate in which both sides seem to have grasped an aspect of the truth, but found themselves unable to find the breakthrough that would allow them to include the insight of the other.

Ultimately God is mystery. Efforts towards intellectual understanding are not sufficient when approaching the supernatural. We must discover it in our lives, reflect on its origins and clear away obstructions that prevent us experiencing it. Even then our human efforts would not be enough if they were not in response to an invitation that is beyond our full comprehension.

The issue remains so sensitive even today that any attempt to express a solution can be seen as valuing one side over the other. Cassian himself was accused of favouring free will and that put a shadow on his reputation that took a long time to remove. Chaeremon's point is that dependence on God's help should not in any way diminish our efforts to make spiritual progress.

CONFERENCE 14

Unravelling the Text

◇◇

Next we visited Abba Nesteros, once a disciple of Abba Anthony and known as a humble man who guarded his tongue. When asked by Abba Joseph how to weight one's words, he had responded, 'When you speak, do you find peace? If you do not find peace, why do you speak? Be silent, and when a conversation takes place, it is better to listen than to speak.'

When Nesteros learnt that we had committed parts of the scriptures to memory and wished to understand them better, he began by discussing the various types of knowledge.

Nesteros: Each field of science has its own system and method of study and the same is true of religion, which has two sorts of knowledge: practical, which concerns behaviour, and spiritual, which contemplates things divine.

Practical comes first because such knowledge can be gained without theoretical study but theoretical knowledge cannot be gained without practical observation.

Practical perfection itself depends on a double system: The first is getting to know the nature of failings and their remedies, the second is to discover the order of the virtues. No one can advance to the more lofty heights without overcoming the lower ones.

Some, like Elijah, and Anthony in our own time, made it their whole purpose in life to seek purity of heart in the silence of solitude. Others came together in monasteries. Some served in the guest house, receiving visitors. Some took care of the sick, others devoted themselves to intercession for the oppressed and afflicted or to teaching or giving alms to the poor.

Each followed the grace they had received while praising and admiring the virtue of others. Since people can advance to God in many ways, each should complete the one they have chosen, never changing the course of their purpose.

To return to the knowledge of which we were speaking, practical knowledge can be gained in a variety of circumstances while theoretical knowledge is divided into historical interpretation and spiritual sense. This spiritual sense can take three forms: tropological (a figurative use of language), allegorical (a hidden meaning) and anagogical (a comparison to make clearer). A fourth can be added to this, the historical sense.

For example, historically Jerusalem is the city of the Jews. Allegorically it is the Church of Christ. Anagogically it is the heavenly city of God. Tropologically it is the soul of humans, and is frequently subject to praise or blame from the Lord under this title.

Of the four kinds of interpretation the apostle Paul speaks as follows: 'But now, brethren, if I come to you speaking with tongues what shall it profit you unless I speak to you either by revelation or by knowledge or by prophecy or by doctrine?' (1 Corinthians 14:6).

Revelation belongs to allegory, by which the things that the historical narrative conceal are laid bare by a spiritual understanding and explanation.

Knowledge is tropological: by a careful study we can discern what is good and what is bad, what is fitting and not fitting.

Prophecy is anagogical: the words are applied to things future and invisible.

Doctrine is historical exposition with no secret sense, it states what is revealed and to be believed.

As for yourselves, if you are anxious to attain the light of spiritual knowledge and growth, you must first seek that purity of heart mentioned in the Gospels. Keep up your reading that you might get practical, that is, ethical, knowledge. Without putting into practice what you studied, that is, purging yourselves of weaknesses and ridding yourselves of the cares of this world, no spiritual advance can be made.

Be careful to practise silence, as one can become proud of one's learning. The first practical step towards learning is to receive the regulations and opinions of the Elders in your heart and endeavour to perform rather than to teach them. In conferences with an Elder don't give your own opinions but only ask questions that are important. Do not presume to teach anyone in words what you have not already performed in deed.

It is one thing to have a ready tongue and elegant language, and quite another to penetrate into the very heart and marrow of heavenly utterances.

The whole of the sacred scriptures should be committed to memory and ceaselessly repeated. This will be beneficial in two ways. When the mind is occupied in reading the scriptures and preparing the next lesson it will avoid the snares of useless thoughts. Besides this, passages that could not be understood fully while trying to memorise them will gradually expand in your mind and their most secret meaning will gradually be revealed.

As our understanding of scripture deepens, the beauty of its holier meanings becomes more apparent. Fortunately the form of scripture is adapted to the capacity of man's understanding. It appears earthly to carnal people and divine to spiritual people.

For example, scripture says, 'Do not commit adultery.' The literal meaning is obvious to all, but for those who have made progress in spirituality it means more than keeping the letter of the law. Fornication is the word used to describe the worship of idols and heathen superstitions. It also has another meaning, the superstition of non-Christian laws and practices. A fourth meaning is falling for heretical teachings. It can be said that departing, in however small a degree, from God is regarded by the perfect man as the foulest fornication.

Cassian: I have been moved by all you say but also greatly discouraged. Because of my familiarity with literature I am often distracted by the songs of poets and stories of ancient battles so that even at the hour of prayer my imagination diverts me from concentrating on things above.

Nesteros: If you can transfer to the writings of the Spirit the attention you have given to secular studies the former concerns will be expelled and utterly rid of. For the mind of man cannot be empty of all thoughts and, if it is not taken up with spiritual interests, it is sure to be occupied with what it learnt long ago.

In any case, a soul that has not been purified, no matter how much it devotes itself to reading, cannot receive or give spiritual knowledge.

Germanus: Many heretics and non-Christians who are entangled in various sins have acquired perfect knowledge of the scriptures and great spiritual learning. Meanwhile, others with the piety of simple faith know nothing of the mysteries of deep knowledge. How then can spiritual knowledge be attributed solely to purity of heart?

Nesteros: Those who are skilled only in disputation and ornamental speech cannot penetrate to the very heart of scripture and spiritual mysteries. Those who have scorned Christ, blasphemed or defiled the Catholic faith, cannot acquire spiritual knowledge. 'For the Spirit of God will avoid deception and dwelleth not in a body that is subject to sin' (Wisdom 1:4).

For what does it profit a man to gain the ornament of heavenly eloquence and the most precious beauty of the scriptures if, by clinging to squalid deeds and thoughts, he destroys it by burying it in the foulest ground?

If you are anxious to attain to that never-failing fragrance of spiritual knowledge, you must first strive with all your might to obtain from the Lord the purity of chastity.

When you are mature enough to teach, be careful of vainglory and do not teach at random those who are not prepared for it. It is right to hide the mysteries of spiritual meaning from such people, but it can be asked, to whom then are the mysteries of Holy Scripture to be dispensed? To use the words of Solomon, give strong drink to those who are in sorrow, wine to those in pain (Proverbs 31:6).

In two situations the teaching of spiritual things will be ineffectual: if the teacher is recommending that of which he has no experience, or the hearer is full of faults and cannot receive in his hard heart the holy and saving doctrine of the spiritual man. However, sometimes, for the good of all, the lavish generosity of God grants those who have not led an irreproachable life the grace of spiritual teaching.

Let us now stop for supper and later talk about the gifts of healing granted by the Lord, as learning should be gained by degrees and without excessive bodily effort.

◇◇

For a humble man who guarded his tongue, Nesteros was exceptionally well informed on the ways of acquiring knowledge and had no hesitation in sharing them. His conference, which goes on for twenty long pages, indicates a high level of sophisticated thinking among the desert Elders. The tradition continued in the monastic schools of Ireland and elsewhere.

Nesteros saw knowledge as either practical or spiritual. By 'practical' he meant becoming aware of our inner conflicts, weaknesses and needs. 'Spiritual' was deepening our awareness and relationship with God.

Here he focuses on the spiritual side and how the scriptures can help us. He describes the four ways in which the scriptures can be interpreted, and from his frequent quotations from the Bible his own familiarity with the Old and New Testaments is obvious. The life of the Desert Fathers and Mothers was based on the Bible. They drew on the Old Testament for its background information and on the New Testament for guidance in following the example of Jesus – his time in the desert, the directions he gave and his giving up all with his death. The ideal always before their eyes was taken from Jesus' statement of his vision in the Sermon on the Mount: 'Blessed are the pure of heart for they shall see God' (Matthew 5:8).

Not all monks showed the same intellectual rigour as Nesteros; their approach to the Bible was more reflective than scholastic. If they did not understand a verse or a passage, rather than consulting commentaries, they read it over and over again, imploring God to reveal the hidden meaning to them. To them it was not a form of prayer but a mystical encounter.

A monk asked Abba Sisoes the Theban for a word of advice. He answered, 'I read the New Testament, and then I turn to the Old.' His spiritual practice was to read scripture from beginning to end, then start again beginning with Genesis. The best advice he could give was to read scripture. 'Scripture will teach you everything.'

In the desert books were not always available so monks like Cassian and Germanus knew large sections of scripture off by heart. Those who could not read heard passages from it regularly and recited the Psalms together daily. However, Christianity is a 'religion of the book', and its arrival in Ireland in the fifth and sixth centuries led to the spread of literacy. Writing and books became a familiar part of life. Most Irish monasteries had a scriptorium in which hours were spent copying and illuminating the Gospels. To quote John Ryan in his Irish Monasticism, 'To the Irish mind an illiterate monk was a contradiction in terms.'

Nesteros finally warns against teaching without fully appreciating what you are saying, being a talkative teacher rather than an attentive listener, and not practising what you read or teach.

CONFERENCE 15

Wonders and Wonderworkers

◇◇◇

After evening prayer we came together again and, sitting on our mats, waited in silence for Nesteros to begin his discourse.

Nesteros: Our previous discussions raised the topic of spiritual gifts. These can be used in one of three ways. Take healing, for example.

The first use is when healing is done for the sake of those in need. Many striking examples can be found in the lives and activities of holy people.

The second use is healing done for the edification of those who bring the sick, and indeed for the whole Church.

The third use is when the gift of healing is given by demons to unfit persons so that others will be misled into imitating their false way of life.

Miracles in themselves are not to be admired; seeming miracles can be done by good people and by bad. Rather they should be judged by the reason they are performed and the most admirable reason for a miracle is love.

We should not be amazed at dramatic cures but rather look to see whether the person who performed them has driven sin out of their lives and made progress in their spiritual search. The power of healing is not granted because of the faith of others but because of one's own earnestness and by the grace of God.

As the apostle says when describing the various gifts – faith, knowledge, prophecy, almsgiving and martyrdom – 'Yet I show you a still more excellent way, that is, love' (1 Corinthians 12:31). It is clear that the heightening of perfection and blessedness does not consist in the performance of wonderful works but in the purity of love. All other things are to pass away but love is to abide forever.

We know that even when healing powers were possessed by our Elders they would never use them unless extreme and unavoidable necessity drove them to do so.

Take, for example, Macarius, the first to find a home in the desert of Scete. He raised a dead man to life in order to discredit a heretic who had come to confuse the simple people of Egypt. His spiritual power would probably have remained hidden if he had not felt the need to save those being led astray.

Such holy men gave no credit to themselves for the powers they possessed. They confessed that it was due to the compassion of the Lord.

This ability to work miracles and signs is not always necessary, or good for all, or granted to all. More important is humility, the mistress of all virtue and the surest foundation of the heavenly building. Love, not the performance of miracles, is the sign of a follower of Christ.

In fact, the greatest miracle is to root out from one's own flesh the incentives of immorality. It is a greater thing to have shut out the devouring pangs of gloominess from one's own heart than to have expelled the sickness of another and the fever of their body.

Learn from Abba Paphnutius. He was famous for the strictness of his life and believed he was free of all feelings of concupiscence. One day some holy men came to visit him and he prepared a porridge of lentils for them. In the process his hand got burnt by a flame. He was mortified and asked himself, why was the fire so angry at me when my more serious contests with temptations have ceased? Joking or serious, he considered the flames as demons punishing him. But if the demons within him were at peace, why were those outside so unruly?

Then he had a vision in which an angel said to him, 'Paphnutius, why are you vexed because this earthly fire is not yet at peace with you, while there still remains in your body some disturbance of carnal motions? As long as the roots of this weakness flourish within you, they will not allow material fire to be at peace with you.

'Go, take a naked and most beautiful virgin, and if while you hold her you find that the peace of your heart remains steadfast, and that carnal heat is still and quiet within you, then the touch of this visible flame also shall pass over you gently and without harming you as it did over the three young men in Babylon.'

Paphnutius avoided attempting this experiment but examined his own conscience and purity of heart. He estimated that the extent of his purity did not yet outweigh the challenge in his vision. He said to himself, 'It is a greater virtue and grander grace to extinguish the inward lust of the flesh than by the power of God to subdue wicked demons that come from outside.' Dealing with the pain caused by the flame of the stove might be easier than dealing with that caused by his internal frailty.

* * *

After telling us this story, Abba Nesteros ended his account of spiritual gifts.

He offered to accompany us the following day to the cell of his neighbour, Abba Joseph, six miles distant.

Religion has long been associated with miracles. People said to be close to God are believed to have supernatural powers or gifts and were sought out for help or intercession at times of need. The ability to perform such miracles is itself a proof of holiness and a precondition for being officially recognised as a 'saint' through canonisation.

Monks undergoing spiritual training in the desert would be familiar with stories of cures and other extraordinary achievements of famous Elders. Even in a place like the Skelligs monks may have been expected to perform a miracle cure for pilgrims visiting them during the summer.

The British monk Gerald of Wales, who was in Ireland in 1183–85, wrote about a miraculous stone outside the church of St Michael on the Skelligs, which, 'through the merits of the saints of the place', provided enough wine each morning for the priests there to say Mass that day.

However, Nesteros had some sobering advice for Cassian and Germanus.

A miracle, or any good deed, should be performed out of genuine love of God and others, and not for any other reason. Miracles are performed to meet someone's need, not to display sanctity. They are to be judged on the basis of the reasons they are done, and those should be genuine concern or love.

Miracles are possible, not because of the faith of the petitioner, but because of the goodness and humility of those who perform them. The holiness of such people should be visible from signs that they have driven sin out of their lives and made progress in their spiritual search.

Besides healing, there are other spiritual gifts such as faith, knowledge, almsgiving and prophecy, but among them love is the greatest because its effects will never pass away.

A final word of advice was to heal oneself first. The story of Paphnutius may be extreme but it brings home the point that before you try to expel demons from someone else you need to check that none remain within yourself.

Cassian knew many stories about miracles performed by holy men in the desert but he showed little interest in them. He claimed he was there solely to learn from their spiritual experience and progress.

CONFERENCE 16

Relationships that Endure

Abba Joseph belonged to an eminent Egyptian family and had been educated in Greek as well as the local language. When he met us he asked us if we were brothers. On hearing that we had long been close friends he decided to talk with us about friendship and relationships.

Joseph: There are many kinds of friendship and companionship which unite people in different forms of relationship.

For some it starts with a recommendation that leads to acquaintance, and from there to friendship. For others it is some bargain or agreement they enter into that brings them closer. For others, it is a common interest in business or science or art. Even robbers in forests and mountains can cherish their partners in crime!

There is another kind of love, based on family relationship, by which members of the same tribe, wives and parents, brothers and children are preferred before others. Even animals share this bond and can expose themselves to danger to protect their young.

But none of these kinds of love, which are common to the bad as well as to the good, can last for ever. Separation, forgetfulness and the busy demands of life can bring them to an end.

The one kind of love that is lasting and does not depend on a recommendation, a kindness, an agreement or necessity comes from a shared desire for growth in virtue. Once it is entered into no passing of time or difference of opinions can damage it. Even death cannot extinguish it.

However, once a friendship has begun effort has to be put into developing it.

Some people cannot maintain a friendship because, although it began well, they did not give equal attention to the purpose for which it began. Their affection was not maintained by the good will of both but by the resolve of one party only. It survived for a period by the unwearied patience of one but was broken by the small-mindedness of the other. Only a friendship sharing the same purpose, wanting the same things and refusing the same things will survive.

To play your part in keeping a friendship alive you must admit your faults, control your desires and strive to achieve closeness in spirit. The Psalms say, 'How good and joyful a thing it is for brethren to dwell together in unity' (Psalm 133:1). This is a unity of spirit rather than of place. Being together does not always mean unity and separation need not destroy unity. Friendship cannot flourish where differences exist.

Germanus: What should be done when one person wants to do what he thinks is necessary but the other does not agree?

Joseph: Friendship demands equal generosity, like-mindedness and purpose. If there are angry disputes it is a sign these conditions are not being met. However, since no one can start from this state of perfection, let us examine what is required to develop fellowship within a community.

First, the foundation for true friendship is putting worldly goods and prized possessions in second place. We who have given up everything already should let no attachment to worthless things come in the way of what is most valuable, the love of a brother.

Second, cut back on your estimation of yourself. Don't imagine yourself as wise and experienced, putting your own opinions before those of others.

Third, even what is useful and necessary should not be put before the blessings of friendship and peace.

Fourth, never get angry for any reason, good or bad.

Fifth, try to try to cure any anger another may have shown.

Lastly, and this applies to all faults, remember we are not long in this world.

Christ said, 'By this shall all know that you are my disciples, if you love one another' (John 13:35). There is nothing more damaging than anger and vexation, and nothing more advantageous than love.

At times we may need help from others. In my youth I had a friend with whom I thought I agreed on all important issues. However, when we began to exchange ideas we discovered differences of opinion to which both of us held stubbornly. It was only when the Elders stepped in and ordered us not to insist on the correctness of our own ideas, but to defer to the other, that we escaped from the divisive forces that threatened to separate us.

The advice of a wise Elder can help in developing a humble and gentle heart, showing us how to avoid darkness and gain the light of true understanding. Even a person who has a keen intellect and much learning can get the wrong notion in his head, while one who seems duller can see the matter better and more truly.

When we speak of love we should remember that not only does it belong to God, but that it is God. 'God is love: whoever lives in love, lives in God, and God in them' (1 John 4:16). It is the Holy Spirit who dwells in us and sows the love of God in our hearts.

Yet there are different grades of love.

It is possible for the love shown to us by God, known as agape, to be directed to all around us. The gospels teach us to love our enemies. But there is also diaqesis, affection shown to only a select group such as parents, spouse, siblings, one's children and those with similar interests. Even then, the degrees of affection may not be the same. We have the example of Jacob, who had twelve sons, but had a special regard for Joseph, treating him with tenderness and indulgence.

Jesus loved all his disciples but John was called 'that disciple whom Jesus loved'. That love did not indicate any coldness towards the other disciples, only a fuller and more abundant love towards John. A richer grade of superabundant love singled him out.

True love, while it hates no one, can cherish some more than others by the reason of their deserving it. While it loves all in general, it marks out for itself some it may regard with a special affection, and even among them some may be preferred to others.

There are also those who, instead of trying to build up relationships, damage them by their obstinacy. When offended in an argument with another, instead of humbly trying to repair the relationship, they go off to sing a verse of psalms as though that will make up for angry thoughts. A well-timed expression of regret is a more effective way of healing their own feelings and softening their neighbour's heart. As Jesus said, 'First be reconciled to your brother, and then go and offer your gift' (Matthew 5:24).

Sometimes a monk will show greater patience and understanding towards outsiders than towards his own brothers because he expects more from them. This obstinate rage of an angry soul causes injury to the individuals themselves, no matter whether it is directed at someone close or distant.

Sometimes it is our reproachful and silent looks, rather than scornful words, that provoke others to anger. It is as if we believed that it is only words that condemn us before others and before God. Our quarrels will be judged not by how much anger they caused but by whose fault they started. It is the purpose, and not the way in which the fault is committed, that must be taken into account.

Often pretended patience excites others to anger more keenly than words, and a spiteful silence exceeds the most awful insults in words.

Some, when vexed or outraged, abstain persistently from food. This is a form of sacrilege, because out of rage they endure fasts that ought to be offered to God alone out of desire for humility of heart and purification from sin.

There are others who practise a counterfeit patience. When, as the result of a quarrel they have caused, they receive a blow, they offer up another part of their body to be hit as a way of practising, 'When a man hits you on the right cheek, offer him the other also' (Matthew 5:39).

Germanus: How can you blame one who, in an argument with a brother, satisfies the command of the gospel and not only does not retaliate but is actually prepared to turn the other cheek?

Joseph: As we said before, we must look not only at the thing done but at the mind and purpose of the doer. The virtues of patience and gentleness cannot possibly be fulfilled by the opposite spirit, that of impatience and rage.

A person who subjects his will to his brother's is stronger than he who is the more pertinacious in defending and clinging to his own decisions. It is the weak in spirit who are quick and ready to offer reproaches and sow seeds of quarrels, while they themselves cannot bear to be touched by the shadow of the slightest wrong.

Remember what the Elders have told us: Love cannot stand firm and unbroken except among those who have the same purpose and goodness.

Germanus: How then can the patience of the good be praised if they cannot tolerate living along with the weak?

Joseph: It is not because the patience of the more restrained will be under pressure but because those who are less able to control their feelings might be encouraged by the tolerance shown to them and daily get worse.

If you want to help keep the peace, when provoked you should try to remain unmoved in speech and heart. If you find yourself under pressure, keep silent. Turn your mind to a previous time when relationships were better or look forward to the restoration of mutual appreciation.

We ought, therefore, to restrain every movement of anger and moderate it with discretion. A fool is moved by anger to seek revenge but the wise person little by little diminishes the heat of their passion and gets rid of it. Unless a neighbour's wrath is overcome at once by amends being humbly made it provokes more anger than what is avoided by taking flight.

What we have learnt from prudent teachers is that those who enter into a friendship for the wrong reasons will not be able to preserve its harmony unbroken. True harmony and union exist only among those whose life is pure, and who share the same goodness and purpose.

* * *

We learned much from Abba Joseph in these discussions on friendship and were inspired all the more ardently to make lasting the love of our companionship.

The advice offered in this conference would not be out of place in a modern conversation and applies as much to married couples as to monks in a monastery. It is 1,600 years old and based on a combination of Greek thought (Joseph had a classical education), Christian teaching and a reflection on the practical experience of monastic communities.

The connection between solitary hermits and monks in community is described in Conference 18. Neither were completely cut off from contact with others or the wider world. In Ireland such contact was encouraged and led to the practice of having an 'anam cara', or soul friend, for advice and support. The Irish 'Desert Mother', St Brigid, is quoted as saying, 'Anyone without a soul friend is like a body without a head.' That 'compassionate presence' could be cleric or lay, male or female.

Here Abba Joseph analyses friendship in classical and Christian terms.

The only true friendship that is sure to survive is one based on a common interest or purpose. Joseph is thinking of a shared wish to understand and practice agape, God's love that extends to everyone. Love is God and God is Love. Our ability to love comes from our bond with God.

Developing such a relationship is not easy. It involves putting the other person first, practising humility and not expecting anything in return.

There is another type of relationship within the monastic community that Joseph accepts – a special affection shown to a few, which does not lessen relationships with the wider circle. He gives examples from the Old Testament and the life of Jesus. Does this indicate that God loves some more than others? If so, is it because they are more deserving or because they reflect his love more? There is an old saying, 'Whom God loves die young'.

Joseph is aware of the psychological battles that can take place in communities, families, groups and the workplace. The silent glare can do more damage than angry words.

The value of having a 'soul friend' was considered essential by many Elders, but even in the desert there were warnings against 'particular friends' with a bond that differed from the expectations mentioned above.

Cassian and Germanus themselves were an example of Joseph's ideal. They had a close relationship for over twenty-five years, based on their shared search for spiritual wisdom.

CONFERENCE 17

Going Further than Planned

After the conference ended Abba Joseph led us to a distant cell where it was very quiet. However, thoughts of the recent discussion prevented us from sleeping, and we moved to an even more remote spot to discuss them.

We recalled that when we set out on our journey we had solemnly promised our Elders in Bethlehem that we would not stay away long but quickly return to our cells.

However, we were learning so much about living a life of perfection from the holy men we met that it would seem a waste not to stay on and learn more. We might never have a chance of coming to the Scete again, yet the weight of our promise to the Elders weighed heavily on us.

We agreed to put the problem before Abba Joseph, who was greatly respected for his counsel and experience. We would approach him after the usual greetings, recitation of psalms and prayers.

When Abba Joseph saw us he asked why we looked so solemn and Germanus explained our predicament.

Joseph: Are you sure that you can get more profit in spiritual matters here in this country? A monk should not make any promise hastily in case he has reason to change his mind later.

When a choice has to be made, what is more advantageous should be preferred over what is not. In this case it would be better for you to undergo the loss of a promise you could not fulfil than a loss that would hold back your search for perfection. A careless promise can be pardoned if it is turned into a better path.

Germanus: We believe that if we return to our monastery immediately we would have failed in our purpose of gaining spiritual enlightenment. Considering the comparative mediocrity of our home monastery it would be a step backwards.

Joseph: In every activity it is the purpose that matters. If your intention is solely to do what is needful and holy then it will not be considered blameworthy.

Germanus: We were not only afraid of displeasing our Elders and disobeying their orders but had foolishly believed that if we learnt anything on our journey here we would be able to implement it on our return home. Now we realise we have not achieved that stage yet.

Joseph: It would appear that, from a desire for perfection, you bound yourselves with an oath. But now a riper judgement intervenes and it seems you have not yet reached the hoped-for heights. If you can show God a clean heart, and the attainment of the original purpose is easier in this country, then the change of plans will not be held against you.

Germanus: What troubled us was the thought that if we did not keep our promise we would set a bad example for the weaker members of our community who might think we were guilty of lying.

Joseph: There are always opportunities and occasions for the malicious. We should not, because of another's weakness, reject what is right. You should explain to those concerned how you made your decision and why you think you have done rightly.

You are afraid that you will be accused of lying. Lying is something different. A lie is like a hellebore (a medicinal but poisonous plant). It can be useful if taken for some deadly disease, but if taken without being required causes immediate death. Take the examples of Rahab and Dalila, who told lies to divert disaster. When any grave danger hangs on confession of the truth, then we must take to lying as a refuge, though it might trouble our conscience. But when there is no urgent reason a lie should be most carefully avoided as if it were something deadly.

Germanus: Such an attitude to lying was understandable in previous times, before the light of the gospel was known. But did Jesus not say, 'Let your speech by yea, yea, nay, nay: but what so ever is more than that is of the evil one' (Matthew 5:37).

Joseph: In the Old Testament too it was clearly stated, 'Thou shalt avoid a lie' (Exodus 23:7). However, it could be used as a last resort to avoid a greater evil, as we have shown. There are many examples in the New Testament. Paul was encouraged to adopt a fictitious arrangement of purifying himself according to the Old Law in order to make himself acceptable to the Judaic population. He himself said, 'To the Jews I became as a Jew that I might gain the Jews, to those who were under the law as being under the law, though not myself under the law, that I might gain those who were under the law' (1 Corinthians 9:20).

For instance, what is to be done when you are observing a fast and a brother comes and asks you if you have eaten? If you say you are fasting, you go against what the Lord commanded when he told us to conceal our fasts from others lest we seem to be boasting or proud. Or when someone out of charity offers you a cup when you pass their cell? Will you refuse his charitable offer?

Germanus: In the first case a lie is unavoidable but in the second, there is no need to tell a lie.

Joseph: It is because of your training in strict monasteries that obstinately prefer their own will to the brothers' needs that you say this. But our tradition is that men who give in to the infirmities of others receive much richer fruits than those who persist in their determination. So it is better to conceal abstinence than display a proud show of truth.

Take Abba Piamun. He lived a strict life for twenty-five years but did not hesitate to accept some grapes and wine offered to him by a brother even though it went against his abstinence, which he had kept as a secret from everyone. There are many examples in scripture of holy people who, to preserve life, to receive a blessing, to show compassion, to conceal a secret or to display their zeal for God, had to tell what could be called lies.

If, in a moment of anger or other passion, we bind ourselves with an oath that clashes with the interests of others, we should consider carefully whether keeping our promise is more important than something good and more desirable. The most respected fathers were never hard or unyielding in decisions of this sort but ready to modify their thinking when sounder counsels prevailed.

Germanus: it seems that a monk should not make any serious decisions lest he turn out to break them or become an obstinate person.

Joseph: That does not apply to the fundamental commands on which our life is based but to those that we can relax without endangering our state, such as strict and unbroken fasts or prohibitions against leaving one's cell. What we must faithfully observe are the fundamental commands for the preservation of love, for which all things else should be disregarded lest the beauty and perfection of its calm should suffer a stain.

The monk ought not hastily to make promises concerning the body, lest he set himself tasks that he cannot complete, 'for where there is no law there is no transgression' (Romans 4:15).

***

Following our discussions with Abba Joseph we decided to stay on in Egypt. After seven years we hastened back to our home monastery and reported to the Elders whom we had kept informed through letters. We were received warmly and allowed to return to Scete to continue our quest.

◇◇

Cassian and Germanus were discovering that progress in the spiritual journey depends on not deceiving yourself when choosing what path to follow in life, when to begin something new, what to leave behind.

That is why even-handed decision-making was one of the first things they were taught (see Conference 2). Responsibility ultimately lies with the individual and their intention, but when discernment has reached is limits the problem should be brought to an Elder or a soul friend. That is what Cassian and Germanus were doing when they met Abba Joseph for the second time.

Should they keep their promise to return to their home monastery in Bethlehem within a certain period or should they stay on in Egypt where they felt so much more could be learnt? There was the added complication of breaking a solemn promise if they opted for what seemed the better course of action.

Abba Joseph assured them that if their intentions were sincere and it was easier to achieve their original purpose in Egypt than elsewhere, then the change of plans would not be held against them. Lies and broken promises should be avoided but are understandable in certain circumstances to protect a better good. While key virtues such as love, purity and righteousness are not negotiable, fasting, abstinence, reading and travelling are.

Joseph accepted that the monastic system in Syria, where Cassian came from, was considered stricter and less humane that that of Egypt. He gave an example of the more relaxed attitude among local monks towards showing hospitality towards unexpected guests while they themselves were engaged in a fast.

Cultural differences were understandable as long as the practice of charity was not neglected. Take lying. In certain societies, bending the truth to save feelings or embarrassment is considered more important than conveying the true facts. This is a practice that is not unknown to the Irish, who are sometimes accused of, or praised for, having a relaxed attitude towards the truth at times. They might not have had to learn it from the monks; it is a very human way of preserving relationships. The circumstances and the intention to be compassionate are what matter. Cassian's flexibility and moderation are again evident.

In Cassian's lifetime monastic vows were not formal. However, stability, or staying close to one's cell, was valued highly and was the reason why he and Germanus had solemnly promised their Elders to return to their monastery after a certain number of years. It was the reason the monks on the Skelligs, cut off from the mainland for months at a time, had no problem remaining in their cells.

Benedict of Nursia (480–543) in his famous Rule would insist on monks taking solemn and public oaths to observe poverty, obedience, conversion of life and stability.

In Ireland the practice of 'stability' was not so strict. Fionan Cam, the sixth-century monk to whom the Skellig foundation is attributed, was active elsewhere in Kerry and as far away as Offaly. There are at least nine Irish saints named Fionan, the founder of Skellig being distinguished as Fionan Cam, 'the squint eyed'.

He was a relative and disciple of Brendan the Navigator (488–577), one of the 'Twelve Apostles of Ireland' who studied at Finnian's Clonard.

Monasteries associated with Fionan Cam can be found on a lake near Waterville, Innisfallen on Lough Leane, Muckross and

Kinnitty. Once he had finished his training with Brendan (a great example of a traveller), he seems to have considered it part of his duty to move on and set up one or more new monastic centres. This practice of Irish monks travelling and founding monasteries led to every town in the country taking its identity from a saint's name and the term 'peregrinatio pro Christo' ('travellers for Christ') becoming synonymous with Ireland.

Colm of Derry was a noted traveller even before he left for Iona. Columban, or 'Columbanus of Bangor', at the age of fifty led his band of twelve Irish monks across Europe, establishing monasteries in the wilder parts of France, Austria and Italy. Today many regions in Europe still honour their own 'local' Irish wayfarer saint. The description 'monk by calling and missionary by circumstance' could be applied not only to Columbanus but to many other Irish 'peregrini' well into the Middle Ages.

CONFERENCE 18

Hermits, Monks and Others

After the lengthy discussions with Abbas Joseph, Chaeremon and Nesteros, all of whom had been recommended to us by Archbishop Archebius, we decided to visit the famous monastery near Diolcos, located at one of the seven mouths of the Nile.

There we were warmly welcomed by Abba Piamun, the senior of the anchorites and their priest. The monastery was located on a height and stood like a tall lighthouse for the area or, to use a gospel expression, a city on a hill. Piamun's ability to perform miracles attracted our curiosity, but we were there to receive guidance from the Elders, not record their activities.

On hearing that we were from another country and had come to learn from the monasteries in Egypt, Piamun was happy to speak with us.

Piamun: Anyone anxious to attain a skill must take the utmost pains and care to study the system by which it works; this applies also to spiritual matters.

We have seen young people coming from your country who go around visiting our monasteries, but instead of adapting to our rules and practices, they stick to the ways they already know. They do not spend time in their cells or seek to practise what they have learnt by sight or from listening.

If they are not prepared to change their method of fasting, their form of prayer or even what they wear, what other reason could they have for coming except to want to escape their own country?

If you wish to learn from our knowledge, you must forget all the rules in which you were trained and in all humility follow what you see our Elders do or teach. Instead of discussing further what you hear and see, the experience of putting it into practice will teach you all you need to know.

There are three kinds of monks in Egypt, of whom two are admirable and the third a poor imitation. First are the coenobites, who live together and are governed by a single Elder; they are most numerous in Egypt. Second are the anchorites, who were trained in the coenobium and then chose to withdraw on their own to the recesses of the desert. The third are the sarabites, of whom we will speak more later.

The system of coenobites arose in the days of the apostles: 'The multitude of believers were of one heart and one soul. None of them claimed what he possessed as his own but all things were in common' (Acts 4:32). At that time there were few who found life in coenobia difficult, but after the death of the apostles the faith of believers began to cool. There were fewer expectations of those from foreign countries who wished to join Christian communities.

Because of the weaknesses of newcomers, keeping personal property and possessions became the norm. Those with the original zeal retired to the deserts to practise what they had learnt from the apostles. As a result the system of which we have spoken developed among those disciples who separated themselves from the growing corruption. Since they abstained from marriage they became isolated from their families and were termed monks or solitaries because of the strictness of their lonely and solitary life.

They are known as coenobites and their cells and lodgings as coenobia. That way of life continued up to the time of Abbas Paul and Anthony and today can be found in the stricter communities.

The founders of the anchorites, or withdrawers, were the same Paul and Anthony, men who lived in the desert from a desire for greater heights of perfection and divine contemplation. They were not satisfied with the progress they had made while living in society and were eager to fight with the Devil in open conflict, in a straightforward battle. They did not fear the vast recesses of the desert, imitating John the Baptist, Elijah and Elisha.

Later, when some of the zeal of the orders of coenobites and anchorites began to weaken, unfortunately a third kind of monk appeared. They broke away from the communities of the coenobites and held on to their own possessions. They are called sarabites. Though they want to be called monks they do not practise discipline, are not subject to Elders and do not keep their traditions. They shirk the severity of the monastery, live two or three together, are involved in business and go around as they wish.

There is also a fourth type of monk, those who started as coenobites but, not wanting to be subject to anyone, built separate cells so they could live alone. Having no one to guide them, their condition cannot improve and their weaknesses deepen.

Germanus: What is the distinction between a coenobium and a monastery?

Piamun: A monastery is just the place where the monks live. The coenobium describes the character of the life and its system, a united community of a large number of monks living together.

I see that you have learnt the first principles from the best sort of monks, the coenobites. You are also aiming at the lofty heights of the anchorite's rule with hearts that are genuine and humble.

Abba Serapion taught us a good lesson. One day a man of simple dress and words came to him. The abbot asked him to offer one of the prayers at the liturgy but he refused, saying he was unworthy. He claimed to be a great sinner and did not deserve to sit on a mat, so he sat on the ground. He also refused to have his feet washed by others as was the custom.

After the meal the Abba spoke with him and advised him to stay in his cell and be supported by his own efforts rather than roaming around. The man was so annoyed at this that he could not hide his vexation.

Serapion said to him, 'You have told us you are a great sinner and did not try to preserve your good name. So how is it now, when I gently advised you, you got so angry you could not cover it up with even an appearance of calmness? Maybe you were hoping we would praise you and say, "The righteous man is the accuser of himself" (Proverbs 18:17)? True humility comes not from a humbling of the body and in words but from an inward humbling of the soul. This will be evident when a man does not boast about his sins, which no one will believe, but when another accuses him of them he thinks nothing of it and puts up with wrongs inflicted on him.'

Germanus: We would like to know how we can develop that calmness of heart so that we can enjoy keeping silent and preserving gentleness of heart. Perhaps that blessing can be learnt only in a remote cell and solitary dwelling?

Piamun: True patience and tranquillity are gained only by profound humility of heart. If it comes from this source, where one resides is not important. It seeks no external support from anything and external attacks will only strengthen it.

I will give you two examples. There was a woman in Alexandria who wanted to develop the virtue of patience so eagerly that she actually created occasions when she would be tested in the hope it would strengthen her patience. She went to the bishop, Athanasius, and asked him, 'Give me one of the sisters to look after', meaning one of the widows the church was taking care of.

The bishop chose a widow who was known for the goodness of her character, but the woman returned after a few days, complaining that the widow was not obedient or cooperative. The bishop was deceived and sent her another widow who surpassed all in wine drinking and quarrelling.

The second widow began complaining and demanding more, so the lady of the house redoubled her efforts to make her life comfortable. She finally learned to overcome the troublemaker, not by resisting her, but by subjecting herself still more humbly and preserving her own gentleness and kindness.

When she felt strengthened by these exercises she returned to the bishop and thanked him for his help in developing the virtue of patience.

The second example is that of the Abbot Paphnutius, who so enjoyed life in the desert that they called him 'Buffalo'. Even when he was still young his gravity and steadfastness so impressed the Elders that they admitted him to their order.

This created a burning jealousy in one of the brothers, who took the opportunity when Paphnutius was at church on Sunday to hide one of his own books in the young man's cell. After the church service he reported to the priest, Isidore, that his book had been stolen from his cell.

Such a crime had never been heard of before in the desert, so the accuser urged that they all remain in the church while selected men search the cells. Eventually the book was found in Paphnutius's cell. Paphnutius, though innocent, acted like one guilty of thieving and asked for a plan of repentance. He returned to his cell and fasted and prayed with more feeling than before. On Saturday and Sunday he prostrated himself at the door of the church and humbly asked for pardon.

The accuser was moved by a deep remorse, so great that even the prayers of the other monks and those of the holy Isidore could not heal it. Only when he finally confessed what he had done was he freed from his torment and the name of Paphnutius cleared.

If we wish to attain Paphnutius's level of virtue, we must lay the same foundations to begin with.

I tell you these stories for two reasons. First, that you might learn to seek a greater feeling of calmness and patience. Second, that you might know you can resist temptations only by the strength of your inner person and not by the closed doors of cells, the isolation of the desert or even the companionship and prayers of saints. Paphnutius had fixed his hope not on external things but on him who is the judge of all secrets, the strengthener of all hearts.

* * *

Our visit with Piamun had heightened our desire to be promoted from the infant school of the coenobium to the higher level of the anchorite's life. It was under his instruction that we made our first start in solitary living, the knowledge of which we afterwards followed up more thoroughly in the Scete.

◇◇

All the discussions so far take for granted that the greatest personal challenge is to experience the presence of God in one's life and actively respond to it. The efforts of Cassian and Germanus to discover how this can be done might give the impression that there is only one way, but this conference shows there were a number of recognised and well-trodden paths.

First, Piamun describes the differences between the hermits (anchorites), living entirely on their own, and the monks (coenobites), who share the same ideals but live together in monastic communities. Originally, as in Glendalough, the monastery was not one huge building but an enclosure surrounding a number of cells, structures for common use and churches. Most of the hermits began their journey in a coenobia, perfecting the basics before going out on their own as anchorites. Cassian's accounts indicate that the hermits were fewer in number but regarded as closer to the ideal because the isolation and simplicity of their lives provided fewer distractions and enabled them to spend more time in deep contemplation.

Cassian and Germanus were at the final stages of their internship and ready to experience the life of the hermit. He warns them of the difficulty of the step they were taking and the necessity of a very unexciting virtue – true humility.

In fact, many of those who gave up the life of a hermit to lead or be part of a monastic community tried to keep the 'hermit spirit' alive for themselves by having an isolated cave or cell some distance from the main monastery to which they could withdraw when they had time.

Even on the Skelligs, a monastic site perched near the top of a granite spike in the Atlantic Ocean, there was a 'hermitage' further up the peak, where individuals could go for a period by themselves.

The community at St Feichin's monastery on Omey Island in Galway had a 'hermitage' on neighbouring High Island, smaller and further out to sea.

In Glendalough, St Kevin's 'bed' or 'retreat' is in the side of a cliff over the lake some distance from his monastery.

Columbanus continued this practice in Europe and had his isolated 'bear cave' several miles from the Annegray community.

Reminders of such hermitages remain in remote locations, known as 'Diserts' or 'Dysarts' in parts of Ireland. They were the closest the Irish could come to the deserts of Cassian and Germanus. In some cases hermits spent the remainder of their life in such isolation, while others used the hermitages for a limited period as places of retreat.

Later, hermits and anchoresses took up residence in walled-in cells attached to church buildings. Examples survive in St Julian's in Norwich, St Feichin's in Fore, County Westmeath, and St Duloch's in north County Dublin. Usually there were small windows though which the hermit could view the altar of the church or give spiritual advice to locals and passers-by.

For those whose life was outside monasteries and hermitages, their parish community provided 'pattern days', local devotions and 'parish missions' as opportunities to put aside daily routines and concentrate on another side of life. Today retreat houses provide space for silence, prayer and spiritual guidance.

Cassian was thinking of the choices facing hermits and coenobites rather than those facing Christians in general. However, just as the hermits 'set the pace' for the monks, the monks who lived closer to the people in their locality became a reminder for them of an aspect of life that could otherwise have been neglected. Those outside the monasteries could never devote the same time or effort to developing their spiritual lives, but they came to share the hopes and values of the monks and adapted monastic practices to their own circumstances.

Because of their austerity and focused contemplation the hermits and monks became the high-performance contestants who reached levels few can achieve, but whose example and experience are at the service of all with an interest in broadening their spiritual capacity.

The Christian call is the same for everyone but each follows their own path; that of the hermit is not for all.

CONFERENCE 19

The Self in Perspective

A few days later we arrived at the coenobium of Abba Paul. Normally over two hundred monks resided there but as it was the anniversary of a former abbot many more had gathered.

When the monks were seated in groups of twelve in the large open courtyard, something happened that shocked us greatly. A young monk who was serving was slow in bringing in a dish. When Abbot Paul saw this, he struck him with the palm of his hand with such a blow that the sound was heard all around the courtyard. The youth accepted the blow with such calmness that not only did he not utter a sound but the quiet and peaceful look on his face remained unchanged.

The sight shook us who came from the Syrian tradition and were not used to this method of teaching. In Egypt such examples of paternal correction were used as a lesson even for those who were advanced in spiritual progress.

In the coenobium we found a very old man named John, who was known for a humility that we had come to realise was the foundation of the whole spiritual structure. For young men it was not easy to remain unconditionally obedient to an Elder over a number of years, yet monks like John could endure it for a lifetime.

We asked John why he had given up his life as an anchorite in the desert for the yoke of the coenobium where he would have to submit to others. He replied that he was unequal to the requirements of the anchorites and had gone back to the infant school to learn the lessons for beginners.

We begged him to tell us something more of his experience.

John: I retain the highest regard for the life of the anchorites. After spending thirty years in a coenobium I lived for twenty years alone in the desert. However, the life of a humble solitary in the desert became too demanding for me and I returned to the coenobium where the goal was more attainable. It is better to be earnest with small promises than careless in larger ones. I have nothing to boast about but I will share my experiences if they might be of some help.

In the desert I was often caught up in such an ecstasy so as to forget the weakness of my body. My soul put aside all external notions and cut itself off entirely from material objects. My spirit was so filled with divine contemplation that often in the evening I could not remember whether I had eaten that day. To help remember the day of the week, every Saturday I laid out seven sets of biscuits in a basket and when they were all gone I knew the week was over.

Rather than going further into my experiences in the desert, I will tell you my reasons for returning to the coenobium. You can judge whether I was right or not.

When I began in the desert, life was very simple. There was no need to plan the day's activities, meals were minimal, storing food was unnecessary, there was no buying and selling. There were no worries about personal needs or those of visitors. There was less danger of getting proud because there was no one to offer praise. Such solitude can be compared to the bliss of the angels.

But the number of neighbours and visitors increased and this freedom was reduced. Previously no more than a single pint of oil and a few lentils were needed for visitors, but now twice or three times that were demanded. Practices became relaxed, and when vinegar and sauce were mixed they now poured more oil over them than was required and an Egyptian cheese was added in. The old custom was to add only a single drop of oil to the meal. The reason was that, if none were added, it might give the impression that the monk was showing off his self-denial. Some anchorites even keep a blanket, using hospitality as an excuse!

The duty of welcoming visitors and conversing with neighbours hinders the anchorite's life and dulls its keenness of heart. The freedom of a hermit's life is lost and his fire of divine contemplation is dampened.

I myself decided to move to the coenobium rather than grow cold in the sublime mode of life in the desert. Even if it meant a diminution of purity of heart I was satisfied knowing that I was keeping the one precept that cannot be less esteemed than all the fruits of the desert. That was, taking no thought of tomorrow and submitting completely to the Abba. As it is said, 'He humbled himself and became obedient unto death' (Philippians 2:8), and 'For I came not to do my own will but the will of the Father who sent me' (John 6:38).

What I would lose in deepest contemplation would be made up for by submission and obedience and not having to worry about my needs. For it is a wretched thing for a man to profess to learn any art or pursuit and never to arrive at perfection in it.

Germanus: From your long and deep experience, could you tell us more about how the coenobite's life differs from that of the hermit?

John: It is hard to find anyone who attained perfection in both ways of life; to find perfection even in one is difficult. However, I will do my best to answer your question.

The aim of a coenobite is to mortify and crucify all desires and, according to that salutary command of evangelic perfection, to take no thought of tomorrow. As the prophet says, 'If you turn away from doing your own will and glorify him, while you do not do your own ways, and your own will is not found to speak a word, then shall you be delighted in the Lord' (Isaiah 58:13).

The perfection of a hermit is to have the mind freed for all earthly things and to unite it, in as far as human frailty allows, with Christ. As the psalmist says, 'I am become like a pelican in the desert. I watched and became as a sparrow alone upon the housetop' (Psalm 102:6).

However, this is not complete perfection, but a partial perfection. Perfection is very rare and granted by God's gift to but a few. It is attained only by those who, with equal imperturbability, can put up with the squalor of the wilderness in the desert as well as the infirmities of the brethren in the coenobium.

The anchorite cannot thoroughly acquire a disregard for, and a stripping of oneself of, material things, or the coenobite purity in contemplation, although Abbas Moses and Paphnutius and the two Macarii were masters of both. It is difficult to say in which mode of life their zeal was mainly shown – whether their greatness adapted itself more remarkably to the purity of the hermitage or to the common life.

There are some who want to cut themselves off from the world completely. They seem to imagine that the main purpose of life is to avoid the brethren and shun or loathe the sight of another. They were not trained in the discipline of a coenobium and are easily upset. While living in the vastness of silence they themselves do not know why solitude ought to be sought.

Germanus: What help can be given to those who leave the coenobium too early, before they get rid of their faults? While living alone, how can they develop long-suffering patience and discover in themselves what is lacking, if there is no one there to point out their faults?

John: God's help is not far for anyone seeking it but we must recognise our weaknesses that we may get help to cure them. If we feel annoyed that a person is late in coming or anxious to get something done quickly, we should know that impatience is still in us. If we are annoyed that someone wants to borrow a book from us, we are still caught up in avarice. If something we read brings up unbecoming thoughts of a woman we should know the fire of desire is not yet extinguished in us. When we compare our own strictness with the laxity of another, pride still governs our minds.

When we recognise the existence of these faults we know that it is only the opportunity and not the passion of sin of which we are deprived. And so, even a solitary person can detect by sure signs that the roots of each fault are still implanted in them.

Germanus: Just as you have exposed the existence of our faults to us, can you give us an indication of how they can be cured?

John: There is always a cure for those seeking a remedy for their ailments.

Those subject to impatience or anger should practise the opposite. By setting before oneself all sorts of injuries and wrongs, as if offered by someone else, we should accustom our mind to submitting with perfect humility to everything that wickedness can bring.

By looking at the sufferings of the saints, and indeed the Lord himself, we will discover that the various reproaches we receive are less than we deserve.

If, at some assembly of the brethren – and there are such things even in the desert – we are silently disturbed by some trifle, we should ask ourselves, 'Are you not the fellow who, while training yourself, thought you would get the better of all bad qualities and fancied yourself able to stand against all storms? How is it that your unconquered patience is upset by the first trial of even a light word?'

With such reproaches we should condemn ourselves and not allow sudden temptations to go unpunished, chastising ourselves with fasting and vigils. We who are forbidden to get angry or seek revenge should not, because of a sudden blindness, lose the brightness of the true and eternal light.

Germanus: The cure for many passions, such as anger and impatience, is to test them by opposing them with their contraries. But what about tendencies towards fornication? Would they be cured by exposing them to the stress of temptations?

John: Your sharp wits and question show you are closely following our discussion.

In the cases mentioned earlier, the presence of other people is not a hindrance but a help, as their shortcomings can test our composure and patience. But in the case of fornication it is different. There we should be depriving our mind of occasions to encounter it. For the young and weak it is especially a concern, and some Elders ban even talk about holy women or certain passages of scripture as they can arouse dangerous curiosity in the young.

For those who feel secure in chastity, there is no lack of tests by which they may examine themselves even by calling up some thoughts. Such tests, however, should not be attempted by those who are still weak; they are more dangerous than useful.

* * *

With this Abbot John brought the conference to an end. It was time for refreshments at the ninth hour.

Many might consider humility to be one of the less exciting or important human achievements, but it keeps coming up in the pages of the Conferences. Conference 20 describes its crucial role.

The discussion begins by bringing the challenge of the previous conference to a personal level. In his account of the daily life of a hermit, Abba John describes how he discovered he had been aiming too high.

His early attempts to live as a hermit had enabled him to reach new heights of contemplation in God's presence. 'In the desert I was often caught up in such an ecstasy so as to forget the weakness of my body. My soul put aside all external notions and cut itself off entirely from material objects. My spirit was so filled with divine contemplation that often in the evening I could not remember whether I had eaten that day.'

However, the difficulty of achieving and maintaining this state taught him his human limitations. It led him to discover his need for support and structure in a monastic community with its authoritarian system.

The focus on true humility begins with the story of the young monk humiliated in public, and John freely admits he was not up to the rigours of isolation. When monks had difficulties in their spiritual progress they were told to reflect on where their greatest weakness might be. If that weakness is not identified it will keep asserting itself and, even if it is finally controlled, it will be replaced by others. This weakness could be as simple as anxiety to get something done quickly, annoyance at someone borrowing our book, pride in our progress.

That is what John seems to have discovered about himself. It could be connected to the great advances he had made in the desert, 'putting aside all external thoughts and cutting myself off entirely from material objects'. This became a source of pride.

John saw the need to place himself under obedience to an Elder in a community because the way to manage a weakness was to confront it with occasions when it would be tested. Being humiliated by unconditional obedience was one way of overcoming pride. The Elders taught that it is no achievement to be sinless if we have no opportunity or enticement to sin. What holds us back is not what we encounter in the world but what is deeply implanted within ourselves.

Pride is a danger because an overestimation of your value can cut you off not only from your companions but also from God.

Germanus felt his weakness was in another area. Once more he brings up the question of sexual temptations. Should they too be tested by putting oneself in a provoking situation? No, was the reply. They are exceptions. Such thoughts should be banished immediately; testing their limits was not recommended.

Humility aside, how high should we aim? Jesus said, 'Be perfect as your heavenly Father is perfect' (Matthew 5:48). John concluded that it was better to do what you can well than to attempt to do something superior that you will never do well.

CONFERENCE 20

Uneasy Consciences

Abba Pinufius, whom we had met before in our own country, was our next instructor. His humility was acknowledged for good reasons.

When Pinufius presided over a monastery in Egypt the talk about his holiness and miracles began to trouble him. One night he fled from the monastery and made his way to Tabenna, deep in the desert. There, rather than opting for the quiet and freedom of a hermit's life, he decided to submit himself to obedience in a coenobium. He dressed up in rags and lay, crying, in front of the gates for many days, begging to be allowed to enter. To test his sincerity he was accused of wanting in his old age to enter just for the food and security. At last he was admitted and given a job as assistant to a young monk in the garden.

There he humbly did all he was told to do and at night went around doing tasks others had neglected. After three years had passed a monk who knew him previously came to the monastery. At first he did not recognise Pinufius because of his clothes and the menial work he was doing, but finally informed the monks they had a famous abbot among them. They, in turn, were full of remorse for having such a low opinion of him and not treating him as he deserved.

Pinufius was dismayed at the honour now shown to him because of his dignity and rank. He felt he had been betrayed by the jealousy of the

Devil. After a few days he secretly boarded a ship and sailed to the Palestinian province of Syria. There he was received as a beginner and novice in the very monastery where the two of us were living. For a while we even shared the same cell. But even there his virtue and merit could not long remain secret and he was brought back to his own monastery with the greatest honour and respect.

It was because we wanted to learn from this famous monk that we sought him out, and he welcomed us warmly because of our previous encounter. Listening to him give a talk to newcomers about the perfection towards which they should strive, we were struck by our own lack of progress.

When we had a chance to speak with him personally Germanus explained why, after listening to him, we felt a great weight of despair. Our weak strength seemed powerless against the challenge facing us. We seemed to be slipping from a low place to an even lower one as we became more aware of our failures. We wanted to learn how to show remorse for our defects and how to make up for them.

Pinufius: Your humility reminds me of the time we shared a cell together and we were mere beginners in the search for perfection. Since then you have learnt much but you speak as if you had made no progress at all.

Sorrow for past shortcomings is indeed important and expressing it is helpful on the road to perfection so I will do my best to describe its purpose or goal.

True regret means never again yielding to the shortcomings for which we try to atone or for which our conscience is pricked. The proof that we have made amends and received pardon is to be found in whether we have succeeded in expelling from our hearts all memory of such desires and the pleasures associated with them.

Germanus: If we expel from our hearts all memory of our faults how can we continue to stir up sorrow for them and make amends? When

I pray I turn my mind to remembering my sins so I may become more humble and regretful for my faults.

Pinufius: What you ask about is the value of showing sorrow for your faults and a sign that its purpose has been achieved.

The remembrance of faults is useful and needful for those who are still making amends. When we are still trying to make up for our lapses and ashamed by the memory of our faults, our tears of regret will help ease the pain in our conscience. If, in a state of humility, we continue to express our regret, the thorns in our conscience are by God's grace extracted from our hearts and it becomes clear that our efforts towards forgiveness are effective. As the Lord says, 'Let your voice cease from weeping and your eyes from tears, for there is a reward for your labour' (Jeremiah 31:16).

There are many ways in which we can make up for our faults. It can be done by daily fasts and vigils and by restraining the desires of the heart and body. However, it can also be achieved through a loving disposition. 'Charity covers a multitude of sins' (1 Peter 4:8). Other means are: almsgiving, the shedding of tears, the confession of sins, humility and labour, seeking the intercession of the saints, the virtue of compassion and pardoning and forgiving others.

It is not good to go back over past sins. It hinders the soul from the contemplation of purity and, especially for those living in solitude, it can entangle them in the blemishes of this world. When the recollection of past sins comes over your mind you must recoil from it in an honest and upright way. It is impossible for the soul to continue with good thoughts when the main part of one's heart is taken up with earthly considerations.

We stir ourselves to praiseworthy contrition by aiming at virtue and the kingdom of heaven rather than by dangerous recollections of our past.

When we have made amends for our failings the very feelings of guilt will be eradicated from our heart and the opportunities and occasions to repeat our mistakes will be removed.

However, besides the grave faults that can be forgotten once they are forgiven, and the inclination for them destroyed and brought to an end by a good life, there are small offences for which counter-measures will never cease. These are the imperfections we commit every day. No matter how carefully we guard against them we cannot avoid them altogether. It will not be enough to have kept clear of the most hateful of sins unless one also secures by purity of heart and perfect apostolic love the fruits of virtue in which the Lord delights.

* * *

When we had finished our discussion Abba Pinufius encouraged us to stay on in his coenobium, but we were drawn to the Scete desert by the reputation of the monks there and continued our journey.

The discussion begins with further examples of humility. Pinufius is an outstanding example of self-awareness and the two young men had no difficulty admitting their lack of progress and the shortcomings that held them back.

How should they express this regret and when could they be sure their weaknesses had been overcome and they could move on?

Already a system was developing in monastic communities to deal with those who failed to keep up with expected standards of behaviour. Spiritual and social lapses were confessed to an Elder in private and a penalty or 'healing remedy' was decided. This was a forerunner of what became known as the Sacrament of Reconciliation. There was no reassuring guarantee of forgiveness involved; that came later with the rite of Absolution. Indeed, many of the Elders were not priests.

So how could you be sure that your fault was forgiven? That was the question posed by Cassian and Germanus.

Pinufius's advice was clear. You will know your offence is forgiven when you have stopped repeating it. If you still feel guilty it is a sign you have not got over it yet. It is better to forget it and be positive. If you feel you must still make up for it, this can be done by daily fasts and vigils. However, it can also be done by helping the needy, forgiving others and being of service. 'Charity covers a multitude of sins' (1 Peter 4:8). Nevertheless, minor daily failings will continue and must be constantly worked on.

The monks brought this approach to Ireland where there was already a system of imposing penalties on those who committed public crimes such as robbery, murder and adultery. If the crime was big enough it could mean the perpetrator being expelled from the community.

The monks adapted to this tradition and added to the list of crimes the intention to harm someone or break the limits set by Christian beliefs and values. For each of those offences an appropriate penalty was fixed and recorded in lists which were passed around to encourage uniformity.

Willingness to confess one's wrongdoings and atone for them was seen as an expression of humility before others and God. It led to the popularity of the 'Irish penitentials', lists of remedies for failings on the lines of the Eight Deadly Sins mentioned by Cassian. Columbanus is credited with two such lists, one for the laity and one for monks and clergy. The latter spelt out rather severe punishments for the lapses noted by Cassian in his *Institutes*. Columbanus and other Irish monks brought these 'penitentials' to Europe, where they had widespread influence and ultimately led to the development of private confession.

An unfortunate consequence of the lists was that the sins came to be regarded as having a reality of their own and to be avoided as such, rather than being seen as the result of mental attitudes which separated the person from their purpose in life, experiencing the love of God.

The lessons of Pinufius and Cassian were taken seriously in monastic communities across Europe and seeped down to the lives of ordinary people during Advent and Lent through fasting, confessing sins, abstaining from luxuries, helping others, almsgiving and penitential exercises. Pilgrimages to sites such as the Skelligs provided opportunities for such practices, and the 'purgatory' of Lough Derg is a living example.

CONFERENCE 21

Utopian or Dystopian?

Our next discussions were with Theonas. While he was young his parents persuaded Theonas to marry because they were concerned about his moral welfare. They believed that the passions of youth were best managed by the lawful remedy of marriage. After five years of wedded life and becoming a wealthy man, Theonas approached Abba John who, because of the high esteem in which he was held, had been put in charge of administering alms. Theonas joined other devout prosperous men in offering tithes of their income to support the activities of the monastery.

John took the opportunity to repay their devotion with spiritual guidance. Thanking them for their generosity in making offerings for the use of the needy, he assured them they would be blessed. By carrying out this service they were fulfilling the old law, by which a tenth of a person's wealth was offered to the Lord.

Some people tried to reduce the amount to be paid as tithes while the more sincere exceeded it. There are many examples of people whose personal generosity went beyond the demands of the law. Those who kept the law faithfully believed their harvest would be abundantly blessed and they themselves rewarded a hundredfold in this world. Yet, not even those who keep the law faithfully were promised perfection.

We who are followers of the gospel are not bound by the demands of that law but by the words of Christ: 'If you will be perfect, go, sell all that you have and give to the poor and you shall have treasure in heaven and come, follow me' (Matthew 19:21).

The Old Law promised no reward in the Kingdom of Heaven but only solace in this life. However, Jesus said that whoever leaves house or brother or parent for his sake will receive back a hundredfold and inherit eternal life. The old law commanded, the new invites and persuades. Which is the nobler?

It is less praiseworthy to abstain from what is unlawful than from what is lawful, and do so out of reverence for him who permitted the lawful because of our weakness. Curses were heaped on those who broke the old law, but of the new law it is said, 'He that can receive it, let him receive it' (Matthew 19:12).

Here the grandeur of the new command is shown by the fact that it is not ordered but exhorted: 'If you will be perfect, go' and do this or that. Moses laid a burden on the people that could not be refused; Paul offered the guidance to those who are willing and eager for perfection. Christ does not constrain anyone, but stimulates them by the power of free will and urges them on by wise counsels and the desire of perfection.

As the word of the gospel raises those who are strong to sublime and lofty heights, so it suffers not the weak to be dragged down to the depths. The law places those who fulfilled its commands in a sort of middle state between what keeps one safe from condemnation due to doing no wrong, but at the same time keeps them away from the glory of the perfect.

So today it lies in our power to choose whether to live under the grace of the gospel or the terror of the law. The grace of Christ welcomes those who go beyond the law, while the old law keeps its hold over the weaker ones as if they are its debtors and within its clutches. The man who is well satisfied with the mere observance of what the law commands will never bring forth fruit worthy of his vocation and the grace of Christ.

When Theonas heard these words of Abba John he was filled with an uncontrollable desire for the perfection of the gospel. He felt he had not only failed to attain the perfection it implied but had scarcely fulfilled the commands of the law. He returned home and related all this to his wife. He suggested they should serve God in sanctity and chastity while they were still young, as no one knows how long they have left to live.

His wife objected. She was still young and needed the support of a husband. If she was deserted by him and fell into sin, it would be his fault. He replied that it was not right to cut oneself off from something good when it became known, and it was more dangerous to disregard goodness when discovered than to fail to love it before it was discovered. The grandeur of perfection was open to every age and either sex, and all members of the Church are urged to scale the heights of heavenly goodness.

He added that the gospel stated that a person should not be afraid to leave house and family for a greater love, and even promised a hundredfold reward.

Even then his wife would not accept his wishes so, leaving all his earthly goods behind, he departed for a monastery where he soon became noted for his sanctity and humility. When Abba John, and after him the holy Elias, died Theonas was entrusted with the management of almsgiving.

I hope no one will think that we have made this up in order to encourage spouses to separate. We do not condemn marriage, we recommend it. As the apostle said, 'Marriage is honourable in all and the bed undefiled' (Hebrews 13:4). However, many holy men have praised Theonas and we wanted to hear more from him. He came to visit our cell during Eastertide and we first asked him about aspects of the festival that puzzled us. Why is it that during the fifty days before Pentecost no one would bend the knee in prayer or venture to fast until the ninth hour? That custom had not been observed in the monasteries in Syria.

Theonas: It is good to accept the authority of the Fathers when we cannot understand the reasons for a custom. But, since you want to know, I will try to explain.

The scriptures say that there is a time for everything, a time to plant and a time to harvest, a time to kill and a time to heal, a time to be born and a time to die. It does not say that any of these is right or wrong, only that when any of them is fittingly done and at the right time they will turn out well. Whether they are good or bad depends on the mind of the doer and the suitableness of the time.

What is the time for fasting? Is fasting good, like justice, prudence and temperance, which cannot be anything but good? Or is it something that is useful but can be omitted? If we say that fasting is good in itself, then partaking of food would be bad and wrong. But the authority of Holy Scripture does not allow us to say that. So fasting is an indifferent act. It brings justification when observed, but does not bring condemnation when not observed, unless it was commanded.

Our predecessors commanded that fasts be observed with consideration of the reasons, place, manner and time, because if they are done suitably it is fitting and convenient; if not, it is foolish and hurtful.

If a man fasted when a brother came to visit he would be guilty of incivility, and when a weakness of the flesh demands a man's strength be restored, going on a fast would not be helpful.

Fasting is not a good in itself, it is a means to a goal and should not be sought for its own sake alone. We can fast to improve our patience and love but we do not practise our patience and love so that we can fast. There are times set for practising it and it has its rules and conditions.

For example, Jesus told his disciples not to fast while he was with them (Matthew 9:14).

Germanus: Why then do we relax the rigour of our abstinence for the fifty days before Pentecost, whereas Christ remained with his disciples for only forty days after his resurrection?

Theonas: Jesus ascended into heaven after forty days and the disciples waited another ten days for the Holy Spirit to descend on Pentecost. So the total is fifty days. This is the tradition handed down to us, and during the fifty days we do not bend our knees in prayer because bending the knee is a sign of penitence and mourning. We also observe those days as solemnities and do not fast out of reverence for the Lord's resurrection.

Germanus: Does this celebrating and eating more than usual not weaken our discipline and our control over our feelings and passions?

Theonas: That interval for refreshment will not interfere with our spiritual progress if we follow our conscience and do not indulge too much. There should be a balance between taming our appetites and undertaking too much austerity. Relaxation at festivals should be useful and refreshing, not harmful or a threat.

Germanus: Why is Lent observed for six weeks in some countries and seven in others, though neither add up to forty days?

Theonas: Seeing you are scrupulous in these matters, I will attempt to answer you.

In the Law of Moses there is the command, 'Thou shalt offer to the Lord your God your tithes and first fruits' (Exodus 22:29).

This applies to time as well as actual fruits. And since there are 365 days in year, a tithe is thirty-six and a half days. So Lent is counted in different ways in different countries. Those who fast on Saturdays observe six weeks and those who do not fast on Saturdays or Sundays observe seven weeks.

With regard to first fruits, many on waking in the morning consecrate their first and earliest thoughts to God as divine offerings, as a sign of serving the Lord faithfully.

The person who has dedicated their whole life to the Lord, and not just a tenth or tithe, will go beyond what is asked. They do not have to worry about relaxing on occasions because they are already doing more than is demanded.

In the early Church there was no Lent because the fast was observed equally the whole year around. But when the early fervour diminished and people began to look after their own wealth they had to be recalled to their pious duty by a canonical fast and constrained to pay tithes. This was good for the weaker brethren and did no harm to those who, in their voluntary devotion, were going beyond the laws.

Germanus: The apostle promises freedom from care not only to monks but to all Christians. So how is it that the domination of sin holds vigorous sway over all baptised?

Theonas: To understand the domination of sin and how to drive it out, let us take some examples. The law encourages people to seek the bonds of marriage. On the other hand, grace invites us to the purity of perpetual chastity. The law says, offer up your tithes and first fruits and share with others. The gospel says, 'if you will be perfect, go and sell all that you have and give to the poor' (Matthew 19:21). The law says, an eye for an eye and a tooth for a tooth. The gospel tells us to forgive our enemies and turn the other cheek when struck.

The height of evangelical perfection raises such virtue above every law and recognises that we are subject only to the grace of the Saviour by whose aid we can attain that most exalted condition.

Those living by the law strive to honour their marriage, use material goods wisely and avoid anger and seeking revenge. However, they are not free from the danger that, because of their association with these bodily concerns, they will be enticed to go beyond the boundaries set by the law and get caught up in sin.

Even a person who considers themselves as baptised or a monk should know that, if they are not yet under grace and seeking perfection, they will be in a continual struggle to stay within the limits of the law. The servant of the law can easily slip from lawful things into the unlawful.

On the other hand, the person who submits completely to the requirements of evangelical perfection will be free from the domination of sin unless their commitment weakens and they settle for less.

Therefore, the freedom granted to followers of Christ does not remove the obligations of the old law nor the requirements of evangelical perfection. It is the aim of him, who by the grace of adoption accepts all those whom he has received, not to destroy but to build up, not to abolish but to fulfil, the Mosaic commands.

Germanus: We are grateful for your detailed description of the role and need for fasting. But how is it that often after a strict fast we awake in the morning feeling no improvement, rather to have sinned again? We can feel so disappointed that we have little energy for prayer.

Theonas: I recognise the sincerity of your question and your desire to reach perfection, not just in outward appearance, but also in purity of heart. Such matters should be discussed quietly and with a mind entirely free from all bustling thoughts. They are not questions that should be argued with empty words, but discussed from the experience of those who are earnest in the search for truth itself. Therefore, let us take up this topic again tomorrow.

◇◇

Theonas's story leads to an enduring question: Is the celibate life in a monastery superior to that of sincere Christians living out their faith in a family and society?

Cassian takes great care to clarify that he is not endorsing Theonas's decision to leave his wife and become a monk. It was still a very sensitive issue in the Church. Origen argued that in marriage the mutual love of the spouses is more important than the desire of one for a chastity that would conflict with the good of the other.

Cassian begs the reader, 'First of all to find me blameless, whether you are pleased or dismayed at this account of Theonas's choice, then you can praise or blame him as you wish.' Yet he continues to explore the idea that in some way a monastic life is of greater value than family bonds and social commitment.

Theonas contends that the Ten Commandments of Moses list the sins that cut us off from God and the community of his people, but the New Testament goes much further. It leads us to eradicate the seeds of sin buried in our hearts by inviting us to love rather than fear God. The Old Testament urges us to offer a tenth of all we have to God the Creator, while the New Testament invites us to give up everything so that we can share in the experience of a loving Father. Jesus set the standard when he said, 'Be perfect as your heavenly Father is perfect' (Matthew 5:48).

Theonas assures us that the greatness of perfection belongs to all, regardless of age, sex or occupation. All Christians are urged to climb the heights of virtue. The paths followed may be different, but all are united in a common desire to live continuously in the presence of God, both in this world and the next. We are responding to God's call to a heartfelt relationship. The abilities and circumstances of each will decide the form their choice takes, but their mission will be the same.

The reason a hermit's life is highly regarded is because its fewer distractions provide more opportunities constantly to experience and enjoy God's presence. However, not everyone is called to be a hermit and few actually reach the hoped-for heights.

In practice the paths followed by hermits, monks and Christians in society differ, so when a choice has to be made between them, honest discernment is important. We need to take into account our real strengths, weaknesses and intentions so we can start on the right path. When in doubt, we should seek the help of a soul friend or an experienced Elder.

Germanus's final question is a reminder that the demands and activities of the body are as real and complex as those of the soul seeking fulfilment. Accommodating both challenges all Christians, both celibate and married.

CONFERENCE 22

The Holy Sinner

Our next meeting was delayed for seven days until Pentecost had been celebrated. Theonas, alert and cheerful as always, thanked us for waiting so patiently. He had being thinking over the matter in the meantime and profited from doing so.

Theonas: A person who dispenses spiritual guidance can benefit twice from a question like yours. They can contribute to helping the questioner and also deepen their own understanding by having to reflect deeply on it. It seems your question is concerned with why we can endure minor temptations while we are relaxed, but sometimes when we are worn out by fasting and other practices we suffer from the disturbances of nocturnal emissions.

There are said to be three causes for such happenings, which occur at irregular and inopportune moments.

The first cause can be too much eating or drinking. Gluttony is to be overcome not just because it is wrong in itself but lest it inflame us with other unworthy desires and emotions. By even-handed abstinence we should not only keep from richer dishes but be temperate regarding more common foods. It is one thing to hope for peace by passive good fortune and another to be worthy of triumph thanks to one's own efforts.

The second cause can be that the mind is empty of spiritual influences and discipline of the inner person. In that case wandering thoughts must be restrained when awake lest the mind be drawn back to them while dreaming,

A third cause, in the middle of our efforts to acquire chastity, is when we are tempted by the Devil in his efforts to humiliate us.

Your concern is that when emissions do occur during sleep it might rule you out from receiving the Eucharist the following day. If the action did not result from an assent to pleasure, and if it was just a natural occurrence brought on by necessity, then we can and should confidently approach that strengthening food.

To be freed from all such seductive illusions we must first of all make sure that once a temptation has been overcome it will not be repeated again.

Then be encouraged by the fact that as the body learns to avoid evil, it becomes more inclined to do what is good.

When our inner self has finally become immune to external influences we return to God as those who have returned to life from death.

By using this approach we will acquire an enduring peace of body. Until that time the unprompted movements of our bodies will make us feel guilty and unworthy to receive Holy Communion. We know of a brother who had great purity of heart due to his watchfulness and humility. However, when he was preparing himself to receive the Lord's communion he experienced nocturnal emissions the night before. To solve the problem he began to avoid the sacred mysteries, but eventually decided to confide in the Elders. They questioned him to discover which of the three causes mentioned already were responsible and agreed it must be the third. They assured him there was no guilt on his part and urged him to confidently participate in the sacred banquet. Once he did so his problem was solved. It was believed that jealousy of his holiness had led the Devil to test him.

However, even when, by the grace of God, we have accomplished a degree of purity of heart we must nevertheless continue to believe that we are unworthy of communion in the sacred body. The reason is that the heavenly manna is so sublime that we humans can receive it only by the gracious generosity of God. No one is able to completely avoid sin on their own, whether the matter is great or small.

Germanus: It was said that none but the holy should partake of the heavenly sacraments, and you say it is impossible for a person to be completely untouched by wrongdoing. Then how can one who is not holy hope to partake in the mysteries of Christ?

Theonas: There are indeed many holy people, but there is a difference between being holy and being without sin.

It is one thing for a person to be holy, that is, dedicated to divine worship. The term is even applied in scripture to the vessels used in the Temple. It is another thing to be without sin. This dignity belongs to one man alone, our Lord Jesus Christ.

Jesus too was tempted in the desert (Matthew 4:1–11), first by gluttony, then by vainglory and pride. However, he fell into no sin and rejected all the suggestions put to him.

St Paul confessed his human weakness when he said, 'I delight in the law of God according to the inner man, but I see another law in my members at war with the law in my mind and making me captive to the law of sin that is in my members' (Romans 7:23).

Germanus: Some would interpret this passage as applying to others and not Paul himself, who certainly attained the highest level of perfection.

Theonas: You are trying to bring me back to a very deep question just when I thought we had satisfied our quest for wisdom. Let us enjoy some silence now and return again to take up this question tomorrow.

◇◇

Returning to a topic that continued to trouble him, Germanus asks how a person who regularly receives the Eucharist should regard nocturnal emissions. If they had experienced an unwanted occurrence during the night would that prevent them from participating in Communion the next day?

The attitude of Christians towards sexual activities at that time had been addressed in Conference 12. There Chaeremon discussed it in the context of a chastity that calls for the successful integration of sexuality into a person's life. When body and spirit are at peace with each other a convergence can be achieved, which allows the person to experience peace and the presence of God.

Chastity was seen as the opposite of 'lust' (fornication), the second in the list of 'Eight Deadly Sins' as described by Cassian. Gluttony was the first. Michel Foucault points out that in ancient Greece the interest in food and diet was far greater than any fascination with sex and this carried over to early Christianity; 'For instance, in the rules for monks, the problem was food, food, food.'

For the beginner, sexual pressures were one of eight distracting impulses they had to overcome if they hoped to relate fully with God. Gaining such chastity calls for abstinence from feelings and activities that would disrupt the balance. This had different implications for the married and those committed to a celibate life, but had similar expectations of both. Despite our best intentions, the body often acts as if it has a will of its own and behaves in an unanticipated manner. An example is the occurrence of unwanted nocturnal emissions. Germanus is reassured that if the action did not result from a desire for pleasure, and if it was just a natural occurrence brought on by necessity, then he could and should confidently receive the strengthening benefits of the Eucharist.

In this conference Theonas lists three reasons why such unsought occurrences happen. Again, gluttony is seen as the basic source. It is regarded as stimulating the other bodily appetites, including the sexual. Effort is needed to control it. Other reasons for such disturbances include slowness in developing our spiritual abilities and distractions laid by the Devil, who is always seeking to divert us from our goal. Theonas offers assurance that each step taken makes the next one easier.

Developing the theme of who is worthy to receive the Eucharist, he makes a distinction between a holy person and a sinless person. The holy are those who are making a sincere and determined effort to develop their spiritual side and that involves trying to avoid sin. If they show regret for their lapses they can and should receive the sacrament, which is like a spiritual medicine. The only sinless person was Jesus. Jesus, too, was tempted but never deceived.

Germanus objects that St Paul was surely an example of perfection and freedom from sin. Even though Paul himself mentions the difficulty in overcoming a certain weakness he must have been referring to others, not himself. That brought the discussion to another level, and Theonas promises to address it the following day.

CONFERENCE 23

Tightrope Walking

The following day we returned to the topic of free will and human weakness. What did St Paul mean when he said, 'I do not the good that I would, but the evil which I hate, that I do'? (Romans 7:18).

Theonas: You suggest that when he used these words, Paul was not speaking of himself or people like him but about the plight of sinners. These passages cannot possibly refer to sinners but only to those who are seeking perfection. They apply to the chastity of those who are following the example of the apostles. What sinners unwillingly perform their wickedness? Who against their will plots against their neighbour? Who is driven by unavoidable necessity to bear false witness or to cheat their neighbour by theft? We are so inclined by human nature to take the easy choice and do what we feel like that we actually look out for opportunities to do so.

It remains for us to measure the meaning of this passage by the innermost feelings of the speaker. What did Paul mean when he compared good with evil? What good could the apostle not do when he wanted to?

He was already practising all the virtues – chastity, prudence, temperance, piety and justice. He taught religion by the lesson of these virtues rather than by words. What then is that one thing that is so incomparably above those other innumerable good things that he wanted it alone?

Doubtless it is that truly good part, the one that Mary chose when she disregarded the duties of hospitality and courtesy to choose it. That one thing is contemplation, meditation on God, the value of which all the merits of our righteous acts, all our aims at virtue, fall short of.

There is nothing else that of itself is enduring, unchangeable and good. Every creature, to obtain the blessing of eternity and immutability, aims at this not by their own nature but by participation with their creator and his grace. Virtues in themselves are good and precious but become dim in comparison with the brightness of contemplation.

Who, when ministering to the poor, or receiving with kindness the crowds that come to them, can, at the very moment when they are anxious for the wants of others, truly contemplate the vastness of the bliss on high? Could even the most righteous and holy of people, while bound by the chains of this life, so acquire this chief good as never to cease from divine contemplation?

Even the apostle Paul himself, who surpassed in the number of his sufferings the toils of all the saints, could not possibly fulfil this, as he himself testified. Despite his merits deserving great rewards, his mind could not help sometimes being drawn away from heavenly contemplation by its attention to earthly labours.

He said, 'What I shall choose I know not. For I am in a strait between two, having a desire to depart and to be with Christ, for it were much better: but to abide in the flesh is more necessary for your sakes.' Out of love, without which none can gain the Lord, he submitted and remained.

Who, I ask, is so alert and vigilant at prayer or singing a psalm, as never to let their mind wander from the meaning of scripture? Who is so closely united with God as to congratulate themselves on having carried out for a single day that rule of the apostle, to pray without ceasing? To some, such lapses may seem trivial and altogether foreign to sin, yet to those who know the value of perfection a quantity even of very small matter becomes most serious.

If a man with bad eyesight entered a house he might be able to see the outline of large items like beds, benches and tables, but a man with good eyesight will be aware of numerous small items among the furnishings. So the saints, those who can see, can detect shortcomings in their behaviour that others, with less clear sight, are not aware of in their own lives. 'Seeing they see not, and hearing they do not understand' (Matthew 13:13).

If we are ignorant of the virtue of being without sin we will see only large and capital offences as important and think we have only to avoid them. If we are free of them for even a short time we imagine there is no sin in us at all.

Those, however, who seek their happiness in the contemplation of divine and spiritual things will be ashamed of anything that distracted their attention for even a few minutes.

Saints who keep a firm hold of the recollection of God and are borne along, as it were, with their steps suspended on a high wire, can be compared to tightrope walkers who risk all their safety on a very narrow path. They know that if they do not keep their steps on the narrow path with care and anxious regulation, the weight of their body may plunge them to an uncaring earth.

They know from experience that the burden of their flesh will not permit them by human strength alone to reach the desired end and so they entrust themselves humbly to the grace of God.

The apostle said, 'I see another law in my members resisting the law of my mind and bringing me captive to the law of sin which is in my members' (Romans 7:23.)

Therefore, aware of this human weakness inherited from Adam, and combined with a divine desire for perfection, the apostle said, 'For I do not the good that I would, but the evil which I hate, that I do' (Romans 7:19).

Germanus: We agree that the saying does not apply to those who are either sunk in serious offences or have advanced to the apostle's level. But it surely applies to those who, having received the grace of God and the knowledge of truth, wish to follow the right path but are carried away by the ingrained lust of their passions.

Theonas: You say that it refers to those who are trying to keep themselves clear of sin. But such people cannot be numbered among hardened sinners. They surely belong to the faithful and holy who are supported by the daily grace of Christ in resisting temptation.

The baptised who have fallen into sin must know that they are either cleansed by the mercy of God and a life of repentance or consigned to separation from God for ever.

Those words of the apostle Paul are rightly applied to those who seek to avoid serious crimes but are drawn away from the contemplation of God by bodily thoughts. Thus they are often deprived of the blessings of true bliss.

It is the mortal body that restrains us from the heavenly vision and drags us back to earthly things. It causes us, while singing psalms and kneeling in prayer, to have thoughts filled with human figures or conversations or business or unnecessary actions.

Whoever ascribes sinlessness to human nature must deny the witness and proof of their own conscience. How can they claim that they are without sin when they find themselves so easily torn away from the highest good? Is there a person who has celebrated even one religious service without the distraction of a single word or deed or thought?

However, we should not suspend ourselves from the Lord's Communion just because we admit we are sinners. Rather we should hasten to it for the healing of our soul and purification of our spirit. Otherwise we could not worthily receive Communion even once a year, as some do who consider themselves undeserving. It is much better to receive every Sunday for the healing of our infirmities and, with humility of heart and faith in forgiveness, to seek the guidance of a spiritual person.

◇◇

This conference, as the series comes to an end, brings us back to the Martha/Mary issue raised at the beginning and in the previous two conferences. Was giving one's entire attention to God's invitation superior to a sincere Christian's seeking to know, love and serve God in a family and in society?

The discussion begins with a quotation from the apostle Paul: 'I do not the good that I would, but the evil which I hate, that I do' (Romans 7:19). For the early Christians Paul was the model of perfection. What was the good that he could not do and the evil that he could not avoid?

Theonas points out that Paul had already set an unparalleled example of chastity, prudence, temperance, piety and justice. What he felt lacking were the conditions to profoundly experience the closeness of God and participate in God's nature. Because of his daily involvement in the churches he had established he was deprived of the necessary peace of mind for uninterrupted contemplation.

What follows is a succinct account of where contemplation can lead. In the present life there is nothing that is enduring, unchangeable or worthwhile, except a profound experience of participating in God's love. Every creature can obtain this lasting blessing, not on their own, but by participation with their creator and his grace. Virtues in themselves are good and precious but become dim in comparison with the brightness of contemplation.

What person, when ministering to the poor or receiving with kindness the crowds that come to them, can at the very moment when they are anxious for the wants of others, truly contemplate the vastness of the invitation from on high? Could even the most righteous and holy of people, while bound by the concerns of this life, be able never to cease from divine contemplation?

Returning to a distinction he made in the previous conference, Theonas explains that all those who are sincerely trying to lead Christian lives can be called 'holy', even if they are not 'sinless'. 'Holy' people are those most aware of their own imperfections because their conscience has alerted them to the truth about themselves. They admit their faults and try to get rid of them. Those who settle for the socially accepted minimum do not even think that they may be on the wrong path and need to improve.

Despite Cassian's efforts here and elsewhere to explain the sense in which the 'life of uninterrupted contemplation' might be seen as preferable to that of Christian service in the world, the debate continues.

The majority of the original Desert Fathers and Mothers were lay people, but as community life developed in coenobia or monasteries, rules were drawn up for them by such as Basil, Benedict and Columbanus. Their lives remained a cycle of prayer, study and work within the community. When it came to providing services in education and health for people in the area, these were performed within the boundaries of the monastery.

It was only much later that the need was seen to extend activities beyond the boundaries of monastery or convent. This meant the rules had to be relaxed. Eventually, from being 'nuns confined to community life', women could become 'sisters', with fewer obligations within the convent and greater freedom to spend time outside serving the poor and needy.

It was similar for men. The desire to reach out to people beyond the monastery walls led to the establishment of 'societies' of priest and brothers who spent less time in communal prayer and study, giving them more opportunities to serve others locally or abroad.

What was expected of the majority of Christians whose lives revolved around responsibilities in society broadly mirrored those of the monks and nuns. While leading more exposed lives and subject to social pressures, they should be aiming more for the ideals of the Eight Beatitudes of Jesus than the minimum set by the Ten Commandments of Moses. If that was their objective, were their commitments to the Christian message and their efforts to seek God not of equal value?

The desert Elders knew from experience that not all were suited to the solitary life of a hermit and many had to settle for what might seem like the lesser aspirations of a monk in community. The same would apply to those who decided not to enter a monastery but to live out their Christian ideals in society. What was important was to choose the path most suited to one's ability and disposition and follow it faithfully to the end. All such paths led in the same direction and the advice given to all was basically the same: what dangers to avoid, what strengths to develop and what goal to keep in mind.

The monks on the Skelligs and the ordinary people on the nearby mainland were closely connected. The monks set an example and gave purpose to the people's lives. In return the people not only learnt from them but supplied them with food, spread word of their heroic efforts and supplied them with new recruits. It would not be surprising if, by the end of their lives, many among the farming and fisher folk on the mainland had achieved, in their own way, a purity of heart and awareness of God equal to that of those living on the rock.

CONFERENCE 24

To Continue or Go Back?

At this stage of our journey our thoughts began to turn to our families and home country. We discussed this concern with Abba Abraham.

We explained that our friends and relatives were people of such piety and goodness that they would not interfere in our spiritual search and, indeed, we could gain from their earnestness. The local people would provide for our bodily needs, thus reducing the time needed for taking care of material matters. In comparison with the emptiness of the desert, the woods and fields of our homeland would more easily provide us with all that a monk would need.

Besides this, we hoped that on our return home, by our example and instruction we would be able to help those we met on their way to salvation.

These thoughts would not go away so we asked Abba Abraham for his advice.

Abraham: The feebleness of your ideas show that you have not yet renounced worldly desires nor mortified your former appetites. The pilgrimage on which you have started is only of your bodies and not of your hearts. If you had got hold of the right methods of renunciation, all these things would have been driven from your minds. 'Every sluggard is always desiring something' (Proverbs 13:4).

If we here thought we needed supplies of worldly goods we could get them also. We are not short of kinsfolk either, but remember what the Lord said: 'He who does not leave father and mother and children and brethren cannot be my disciple' (Luke 14:26). If we were deprived of the protection of our parents there would be no shortage of princes of this world who would be happy to minister to our necessities. However, scripture says, 'Put not your trust in princes' (Psalm 146:3).

Those who are anxious over the purity of the inner person should not seek fertile districts where their minds are troubled by the task of cultivating them. We delight only in this squalor, preferring this dreadful and vast desert where we pursue no temporal gains but the eternal rewards of the spirit. For it is but little for a monk to have once made his renunciation unless he continues to renew it daily.

We need continually to be on our guard. There are monks, in the deserts of Calamus or Porphyrion, seven or eight days' journey into the deepest wilderness, who are devoted to agriculture and not confined to a cloister. Whenever they come here to Scete they find it difficult; they are like beginners who had never given the slightest attention to the exercise of genuine solitude.

They cannot endure the peace and quiet of our cells and feel obliged to leave. The emotions of their inner person have not been tamed and they have not learnt how to quell the tempests of their thoughts through persevering effort. They toil day after day in the open air, moving about in empty spaces, but only in the flesh, not in the heart. Unknowingly they long for many things. They cannot put a check on the vague discursiveness of their minds nor bear any sorrow of spirit. They pour forth their thoughts endlessly as their bodies move here and there. Continual silence is unendurable. When it comes to working hard in the countryside they never tire, but they are worn out by the quiet and confinement of the cells.

Even those who live in cells can be oppressed by anxieties that dash here and there like wild horses. When their minds roam abroad in that way they may enjoy some short satisfaction, but if they try to rein in their thoughts again the struggle is harder because they have developed a habit of drifting.

A monk's whole attention must be fixed on one point: the recollection of God. Just as a man trying to build an arch must use exact measurements extending from a fixed central spot, so a monk's life must be based on God as its centre or the point towards which his compass always directs him.

Germanus: We appreciate what a monk tries to achieve in his cell. However, we are not clear on why we should avoid the regions in which our relatives live. If experienced and learned men like you can live in your own country, and even near your home village, why should doing so be considered bad for us?

Abraham: Sometimes we see bad precedents taken from good things. If a man tries to do the same thing as another but without having a clear purpose in mind, he can be deceived. If the young Saul had used the same weapons and armour as the giant Goliath he might not have won the fight. Each of us has to first carefully consider the measure of our own powers and, in accord with its limits, to choose the system that is likely to suit our purpose.

We do not assert that, because the anchorite's life is good, it is therefore suited to everyone. For many it may not only be useless, it might even be injurious. The same is true of life in the coenobium. The situation of your country and of this one must be weighed against each other.

We have lived here and our purpose has been tested for many years. If we see that you are our equal in virtue and constancy, then you too need not avoid the nearness of your kinsfolk and brethren.

To give you an idea of how you can test your strength I will give you the example of Abba Apollos. One night his own brother came to the old man and asked for his help in rescuing an ox from the swamp. The old man replied, 'Why did not seek the assistance of our younger brother, whose house you passed on the way here?'

The man, thinking that the old monk was losing his mind and had forgotten that their younger brother had died, replied, 'How could I summon one who died fifteen years ago?'

Abba Apollos replied, 'Don't you know that I too have been dead to this world for twenty years and that I can't rise from my tomb in this cell to give you any assistance in what belongs to the affairs of the present life? Christ is so far from allowing me ever so little to relax my purpose of mortification on which I have entered that I could help you extricate your ox, that he did not even permit the very shortest intermission of it for my father's funeral, which would have been undertaken much more readily and piously.'

So you can now carefully consider whether you can preserve such strictness with regard to your kinsfolk. When you are of the same mind as him, living in the same neighbourhood as your family will not hurt you.

Germanus: On this subject you have certainly left no room for disagreement! We could not possibly wear clothes like these or go barefoot in our own country. Neither would it take the same labour to procure our daily needs. Here we have to fetch water, slung on our necks, from three miles away. Shame on our part, and on theirs, would prevent us from doing so.

However, how would it affect our plan of life to have our needs met by them and not have to be concerned about preparing our own food? That would give us more time to devote ourselves entirely to reading and prayer.

Abraham: I will not give you my own opinion on this but that of blessed Anthony.

A monk said to Anthony that the anchorite system was not to be admired since it required greater virtue for a man to practise the ways of perfection among men than in the desert on his own. Abba Anthony asked him where he lived himself. He replied that he lived close to his relatives who provided him with all he needed so he was spared daily work and could devote all his time to reading and praying without distraction.

Anthony asked, 'Do you grieve over their concerns and misfortunes in the same way as you rejoice over their good fortune?'

He admitted that he shared in both.

'You should know,' responded Anthony, 'that in the world to come you will be judged along with those with whom you have been affected by sharing in their gain or loss, joy or sorrow.'

The holy Abba went on to explain that this lukewarm mode of life would continually drag down the monk's mind to earthly things. He would be deprived of the fruits of his own hands and the reward due to his own exertions. He would be deprived of the opportunity to provide for his own needs as the apostle taught and practised himself (2 Thessalonians 3:7).

Our community had the protection of kinsfolk, yet we prefer abstinence to riches and work to obtain our daily needs. We put that laborious poverty before idle meditations and fruitless reading. If the apostles had taught the opposite we would have followed them gladly. Our predecessors had laid down that anything taken as daily food ought to be prepared by the labour of their own hands.

The blessed Anthony taught us to shun the pernicious allurements of relatives and all who would charitably provide their food. We prefer the sandy wastes to fruitful soil that might distract us to cultivating it and entice us to forget the chief service of our heart, rendering it useless for spiritual aims.

And since you are eager to return to your own country and offer spiritual assistance to the people there, I will tell you a story about Abba Macarius.

Macarius told this to a young man with questions similar to yours. In a certain city lived a very clever barber. He charged three pence for a shave and, after deducing the cost of his food and other necessities out of his earnings, each day still had a hundred pence to put in his pocket.

He came to hear that in another city a barber was charging twelve pence per customer. He thought to himself, 'How long shall I be satisfied with this beggary when I could go to that city and make a fortune?'

So, getting together his implements and spending all he had gathered on the expenses for the journey, he set off for that city. On the day of his arrival he received from everyone the payment he had heard about and in the evening, seeing he had earned so much money, he went to the butcher's to buy food for his supper. However, the prices were so high he ended up with little food and no money.

He thought this over and decided to return home where the profits were enough to enable him to provide for his old age.

It is better to continue to aim at very slender profits from which no worldly cares can detract, than make profits that are absorbed by the demands of secular life. So it is with those who, while in need of teaching and instruction themselves, waste by impatience and rude manners whatever they gain by instructing others. While they fancy that they can make large profits by instructing others, they are actually holding back their own improvement.

Germanus: Your story is very apt, but could you tell us how such thoughts creep in and take hold? Only those who know the origin of a disease can cure it.

Abraham: All faults have one source and origin but different names according to the aspects of the spirit that it infects. When a virus seizes the head, it cause a headache, in the ears an earache and when it spreads to the joints it causes gout. The three powers of the soul are reason (logikon), passion (qumikon) and desire (epi qumhtikon) . When the force of noxious passion infects them the names of the fault that appears is given in accordance with the power affected.

If it hits the intellect it will produce vainglory, conceit, envy, pride, presumption, strife and heresy.

If it has wounded the passions it will give birth to rage, impatience, sulkiness, frustration and cruelty.

If it affects the desires it will be the parent of gluttony, fornication, covetousness, avarice and earthly desires.

If you fancy that you can scale the heights of perfection and actually teach others, you need to look at vainglory and its origin in the rational part of your mind. It can be healed by the judgement of right discretion and the virtue of humility. It is difficult for each of us to heal our soul and admit with the deepest feeling that we are far removed from the right to teach and still need the help of a teacher.

The rational part of the soul is the weakest and the first to be attacked by temptation. The remedy for it is true humility.

Germanus: You have revealed to us that our reason for wishing to return to our country, that it would be to our spiritual advantage, was an illusion and mistake. But we also felt that if we stay here our solitude and silence will often be broken by the arrival of visitors, an intrusion that would not happen in our homeland.

Abraham: Never to be visited by others is a sign of unreasonable strictness and great coldness. If you become known for your great love of God and follow God, who indeed is love, many will flock to you and want to meet you. As the Lord said, 'A city built on a hill cannot be hidden' (Matthew 5:14).

The Devil reduces the spiritual service that monks can offer by promising them greater gain if they withdraw to more remote and vaster deserts where monks of great holiness and humility reside. However, when they have separated themselves from the Elders and gone off on their own to those distant areas they will find nothing of what they had dreamed.

They will no longer benefit from the rare and spiritual visits of the brethren but rather be daily interrupted by worldly folk, who will prevent them from returning even to the moderate quiet of the anchorite's life.

The refreshing periods of relaxation and courtesy, brought about by the arrival of brethren, are useful for the body as well as the soul. Even for those of great experience and perfection, if the strain and tension of the mind is not lessened by some form of relaxation, they will fall into coldness of spirit or a deterioration of bodily health. Such visits remind us of the advantages of retiring to the desert, give us an opportunity to refresh the body and show us the advantages of kindness such as experienced by the evangelist John.

It is told that when John was gently stroking a partridge one day, he saw a philosopher approaching him in the garb of a hunter. The man was surprised that a man of such fame and reputation as John should be engaged in trivial pastimes.

'Are you not the famous John?' he asked. 'Why do you occupy your time so wastefully?'

John replied, 'What is that you are carrying in your hand?'

'A bow,' the man responded.

'And why,' asked John, 'do you not carry it bent everywhere you go?'

The man explained that if he did that the bow would lose its stiffness and become useless.

John countered, 'Do not let the sight of my short relaxation of mind disturb you. If it is not occasionally relieved its spirit would lose its spring and be unable, when needed, to follow what was right.'

Germanus: Could you also explain to us the saying, 'My yoke is easy and my burden light'. The apostle says, 'All who will live godly in Christ suffer persecutions' (2 Timothy 3:12). Such persecution cannot be easy and light.

Abraham: From our own experience we can answer that. What can injure a person who practises perfect renunciation, voluntarily rejects for Christ's sake all the pomp of this world and considers all of its desires as nothing?

What effort, or hard command of an Elder, can disturb the peace of mind of a monk who has no will of his own but to do the will of God? What persecution will frighten the one who always rejoices together with the apostles in their sufferings and longs to be counted worthy to suffer the same shame for the name of Christ?

If we feel that the yoke of Christ is neither light nor easy it is because of our want of faith and our slackness. We fight against the words of Jesus, 'If you will be perfect, go sell all that you have and come follow me' (Matthew 19:21).

When the Devil wants to sever us from spiritual delights he will diminish these or deprive us of them. Caught up in the chains of property and substance we will not have perfect humility or be able to cope with dangerous pleasures.

But if we commit ourselves completely, all the trials of this present life will disappear and we will not only become patient but experience real pleasure.

How is it that the exceeding lightness of the divine burden becomes heavy if not because in our obstinate presumption we despise him by whom it was borne?

The person who truly gives up this world, takes up Christ's yoke and learns from him, will be trained in the daily practice of enduring wrong and remain ever undisturbed in temptations.

The Lord promised that those whose renunciation is perfect will receive a hundredfold not only in the next life but in this one as well. They will receive from those who are joined to them by a spiritual tie a love which is a hundred times better. Love between parents, children and siblings is regrettably short-lived and easily broken.

Monks alone maintain a lasting union in intimacy and possess all things in common, as they hold that everything that belongs to the brethren is their own and everything that is their own is their brethren's. If then the grace of our love is compared to those affections where the bond of union is a carnal love, certainly it is a hundred times sweeter and finer.

And instead of that joy which a person experiences from the possession of a single field or house, they will enjoy a delight in riches a hundred times greater if they pass over to the adoptionship of children of God and possess as their own all things that belong to the eternal Father.

Formerly I had a wife in a domestic setting, now I have the dignity of holiness and the true love of Christ. Then I had but one wife, but Christ promised that those who left their family for his sake would receive a hundredfold. No matter what part of the world you go to, instead of just one set of parents and siblings you will have many parents and brethren bound to you by a still more fervent and admirable affection.

What we will get back is what we have given – offering all we have and ourselves voluntarily in the service of the brethren. Those who prefer to receive attention from the brethren rather than give attention to them will continue to be burdened by this slackness. The Kingdom will be gained not by the careless but by the violent.

The violent are they who show a splendid violence, not to others, but to their own soul by depriving it of all delights in things present. They promise, 'Not as I will, but as you will' (John 6:38). That quality can be seen in those who live in coenobia and are governed by the rule of the Elders, not doing anything of their own will but depending on the will of the abbot.

Finally, do those who faithfully serve Christ not receive a hundredfold? Many of them are humble folk and have even known slavery because of their service in Christ but no one who knows them doubts their nobility or scorns their origin.

Abba John of Lycus came from obscure parents but is now highly honoured even by those who hold the reigns of the empire and the world in their hands. They come from distant lands for his advice and entrust to his prayers and merits the crown of their empire, the safety of the state and the fortunes of war.

* * *

In this discussion Abba Abraham showed us the shallowness of our thinking. He revealed the origin of our illusions and kindled in us the desire for true mortification.

We hope that others too will be inflamed, and that beneath the embers of our words they will find and fan the glowing thoughts of the greatest Fathers.

We have offered these words, not presuming that we can add to your own zeal, but that your authority with your students might be greater if, in addition to the precepts of the greatest and most ancient fathers, what you teach may be supported not by the dead sound of words but by your own living example.

In the late twelfth century a painful decision was made on the Skelligs. The main body of monks left for the mainland, settling in Ballinskelligs (Town of the Skelligs), over thirty miles away. Why did they leave? Perhaps they went through a discernment process such as Cassian and Germanus did in this final conference, though their problems were more urgent than those of the two young men.

The thoughts of Cassian and Germanus had turned to their homeland. Had they not done enough? They had investigated carefully, their thinking had changed and they felt they were moving in the right direction. Was it not time to return to the world they had left and use their new understanding to help others on the same journey?

Abba Abraham pointed out their self-deception. Their concerns about security, availability of supplies, more time for prayer and opportunities to help relatives showed they had not yet fully renounced worldly desires nor reduced their former appetites.

He offers them words of encouragement. The Lord promised that those whose attachment to spiritual progress is genuine will receive a hundredfold. You will get back what you have given. The Kingdom is gained only by commitment and persistence.

Remember, he told them, that your chosen path should not cut you off from others entirely. If you stay in one place you will get close to the people and they will become neighbourly to you. Unreasonable strictness in avoiding contact is not healthy. Indeed, if you are living up to the standards expected of you, people will be curious and come to learn from you.

Cassian and Germanus were reassured and stayed on. There is no record of their ever returning home.

CONCLUSION

A Lost Inheritance?

Gerald of Wales (1146–1223), who lived at that time, said the monks left the Skelligs because a major climatic shift with more violent storms and harsher weather made the rock uninhabitable. Would monks trained in the desert discipline have left for that reason alone?

Another major shift was taking place in Ireland during that period. Malachy of Armagh (1094–1148) was prominent in a movement to bring the monastery-led Irish Church into conformity with the bishop-led and parish-centred Church in Europe. He strengthened the diocesan system and renovated the practices of marriage, confession, confirmation and liturgy.

To promote the changes he encouraged a more 'modern' type of monastic life and invited a number of new religious foundations to Ireland. Among them were the Canons of St Augustine. Though based on the monastic rule of Augustine, a contemporary of Cassian, they were further committed to pastoral or parish ministries and were responsible to the local bishop, rather than their abbot.

By the end of the twelfth century a community of the Augustinian Canons existed in Ballinskelligs on the coast of the Iveragh Peninsula. It was closely associated with Skellig Michael and it seems that the last monks of the Skelligs retired there. The new system of Church reform had little room for independent Skellig-like communities and the number of monks diminished.

Malachy also introduced a strict branch of Benedictines, the Cistercians, in an effort to 'reform' the pliant practices of the Irish Church and society. A number of reform synods were held before and after the Norman conquest of 1169. Such attempts to bring centralisation and a stricter legal structure to Church and society appealed to the newcomers who were determined to unify the country on the lines of their own progressive feudal system. Customs originating in the clan or tuath-based Irish system, such as permitting multiple marriages and weddings with close relatives, were considered uncivilised and were condemned with strong language in Canterbury, the Cistercian headquarters at Clairvaux and Rome. Blame was put on the Irish Church for being too lax.

Despite the reforms introduced by the synods and Normans, Irish society as a whole continued on traditional lines over the following centuries. The spirit of the Desert Fathers and Mothers lingered on and held society together in a tumultuous period of territorial conflicts. Places like the Skelligs continued to symbolise the early heroic spirit of Irish Christianity, providing both inspiration and reproach.

Skellig Michael itself was occupied by individual hermits during the medieval period and the Canons encouraged pilgrims to go there. The rock remained a pilgrimage centre until the dissolution of the Ballinskelligs priory in 1578.

The new forms of monastic life introduced from abroad, with monks sheltering in tall, fortress-like complexes rather than scattered cells, still managed to preserve some of the old spirituality. After their suppression during the Protestant Reformation, only small groups of Canons survived in the countryside to support the ordinary people.

When deep-rooted change finally came to Ireland it had the backing of both Church and society. As the country began to recover from the disaster of the Great Famine of 1845–52, and a degree of religious freedom was granted, Irish priests educated in the new devotional spiritualties of Europe returned home to spark a revival.

For religious and political reasons, Ireland had been slower than the rest of Europe to experience the emergence of a lower middle class that sought respectability and an equivalence with those to whom until recently they had been forced to defer. Protective of their new economic and social status, they were conservative in moral and political matters while keen to conform to new fashions and social conventions. They valued privacy, respectability, education and progress.

From this background a new spirituality emerged, first on the Continent and later in Ireland. It was personal, theologically-reasoned, dutiful and centred on the parish church. Enthusiastically spread by priests returning from studies or escaping persecution in France, Italy and Spain, it found expression in new parish churches, solid buildings in the neo-classical Roman style. Private forms of devotions were introduced that replaced time-honoured practices such as 'patterns', pilgrimages and wakes. The respect shown for the holy men and women of old, whose memory survived in the names of so many towns and villages, was redirected to contemporary European saints.

This new spirituality and respectability enabled the Church to evolve and earn a unique place in Irish society for the next hundred years. Without much effort, in a remarkably short period, it succeeded in extinguishing memories of the previous tradition. Today's generation visiting the Skelligs would have difficulty in understanding the life once lived there. Like the Norse pirates twelve hundred years before them they might have trouble understanding what made people want to live in such a harsh place. What did they hope to achieve there, cut off from everyone else? Why were they confined to such tiny cells?

Cassian still provides the answers.

First, the motivation – why did they go there?

The three reasons given by Abba Chaeremon in Conference 11 for doing what is of greatest benefit and avoiding what holds back personal development provide as good an explanation as any.

The three incentives for re-examining one's lifestyle were fear of hell, hope for the Kingdom of heaven, and the love of God. They reflect, in a curious way, the virtues of faith, hope and love. They first two have value if they lead to the third.

The first is a faith that sees God as judgemental, punishing those who break the commandments.

The second looks forward to a reward for their effort, in this world and the next, from an all-powerful creator God.

The third see God as the answer to the human need to love and receive love, both human and divine. It wants to understand what unconditional love means and, in the process, live life to the full.

To use Chaeremon's words, there is a great difference in being a fearful servant or a hopeful mercenary and seeing oneself as an adopted child of God, with no sense of fear or greed. The experience is that of a father's kindness, with no doubt that all that the father has is ours.

It is possible to move from the first motive to the second and on to the third. However, it is only when we accept that God has loved us first that we can begin to move towards loving God for the sake of nothing but that love alone.

This was the simple message of the gospels that inspired Cassian, the monks on the Skelligs and all who followed the desert tradition. They wanted to experience what was possible.

Why then did they cut themselves off from everyone and any chance of being of service to others in society?

The desert seekers discovered that no progress could be made until three requirements had been met. It meant isolating themselves until the task was completed.

The first challenge was in clarifying their attitude towards what the world has to offer in terms of wealth, power, popularity and ambition. If a desire for any of these dominated their thinking they would be unable to advance any further as Christians.

The next concerned feelings, desires, weaknesses and bonds, which are part of human life but can become obstacles in carrying out a commitment. They should not be allowed to prevent a person from being fully open to God and others.

The third requirement was to give time to study and reflection as a preparation for contemplation and constant awareness of God's presence.

To many this approach may appear restrictive, but to the monks it promised freedom.

Why did the monks live in such tiny and uncomfortable cells?

The Elders said, 'The cell will teach you everything'.

For the early hermits this meant building a hut in the desert and staying there. Later, others found their cells could be closer than they thought.

In their remote cells the monks prayed and worked, making such things as rush baskets which they could sell for food. In their cells they sat before God, experiencing his presence. There they had to confront their weaknesses and failings; there was no one else to blame. They were told that, rather than protecting themselves from the world, they were protecting the world from themselves. In their cells they tried to clear up their anger and contempt, to create an atmosphere of love and compassion that could later be shared with others.

Abba Serapion's advice to newcomers was, 'Son, if you want to make progress, stay in your cell, pay attention to yourself and your task. Going outside will not be as much benefit as sitting still.'

The beehive cells on top of the Skelligs were perfect for that.

Inevitably Germanus spoke up for those who find this whole approach to life intimidating and even irrelevant.

His questions anticipate what many would ask today: Is this attitude not out of touch with the real world? At a time when so many urgent causes call out for attention how can such a passive attitude be justified?

In the first conference this unease was expressed in the Martha/Mary story and it emerges again and again in later discussions. In what way could it be shown that a time-consuming commitment to spiritual matters is in any way superior to that of the Christian serving God in the world?

Cassian implies that while the life of a hermit does give more opportunities for uninterrupted prayer and contemplation it is not suited to everyone. Some hermits even gave up their solitary life to live in a monastic community because of their need for spiritual and human support.

What the hermits and monks can offer the outside world is to be a 'lighthouse on a hill', providing direction, inspiration and encouragement. Admittedly, not all within the monastery immediately became 'saints'. Cassian's *Institutes* listed common faults that needed constant correction. When suggesting that young monks seek out someone worthy of imitation, he warned them that such good example 'will come from a few, and indeed from one or two, but not from the many.' Within the community shortcomings could not be concealed for long and had to be faced every day. The sight of 'holy men' struggling with their weaknesses was reassuring.

While the wider population welcomed the inspirational and highly motivated monks among them, they were also relieved that they were not expected to climb to such lofty heights themselves.

What the monks provided was a reminder that life has meaning beyond the concerns of daily life and it can be discovered only by going beyond such everyday anxieties. The austerities practised in monasteries showed that human weaknesses have to be faced and checked. Left unattended, they can take over a life and restrict it.

As the monasteries opened up to students and visitors they became part, if not the centre, of the local community. The monks visited villages, explaining their life and practices to the people. Their Bible stories added to folklore. Local 'pagan' practices were Christianised and the Christian faith enriched in the process.

Soon the local people were adapting the rhythm and practices of the monasteries to their own lives. They abstained from meat on Fridays, fasted in Advent and Lent, kept vigil at Christmas and Easter and celebrated the feasts of the saints. There were designated times to grieve and to rejoice. Prayers were short but frequent, blessings to remind them of God's presence around them. Such practices have often been neglected in history books seeking economic narratives but they gave meaning, purpose and dignity to the daily life of ordinary people.

In 1996 UNESCO included Skellig Michael on its list of World Heritage Sites, 'on the basis of cultural criteria and considering that the site is of outstanding universal value being an exceptional and in many aspects a unique example which illustrates, as no other site can, the extremes of a Christian monasticism characterising much of North Africa, the Near East and Europe'.

It is a memorial to the Irish heroic spirit, the inspirational life of the Desert Fathers and Mothers and the efforts of John Cassian and his Irish disciples, more pilgrims than penitents, to keep that spirit alive.